CHURCH VOCATIONS
A New Look

CHURCH VOCATIONS
A New Look

Murray J. S. Ford
Judson Press, Valley Forge

CHURCH VOCATIONS — *A New Look*

Copyright © 1971
Judson Press, Valley Forge, Pa. 19481

Unless otherwise indicated, the Bible quotations in this volume are in accordance with the Revised Standard Version of the Bible, copyright 1946 and 1952 by the Division of Christian Education of the National Council of the Churches of Christ in the United States of America, and are used by permission.

International Standard Book No. 0-8170-0544-7
Library of Congress Catalog Card No. 74-160252

Printed in the U.S.A. 73-6968

Contents

Preface

I am indebted to many people who have been eager to discuss the matter of recruitment for ministry with me. In addition to those whose names cannot be included here, Mrs. Jean Parker, Associate Secretary of the Board of Colleges, United Church of Canada; Mrs. Doreen Place, formerly Secretary of the Committee on Christian Vocations of the Canadian Council of Churches; my esteemed colleague Professor L. A. Tupper; and Dr. Ross Snyder, of the Chicago Theological School, have been most generous with time and interest. My secretary, Miss Irene Flett, has patiently typed the manuscripts from very indifferent script.

This book is dedicated to all young persons who are struggling to decide on their vocational future.

Introduction—Ever Want to Say Something?

At the annual Canadian National Exhibition in Toronto the Canadian Council of Churches sponsors a booth. In recent years the emphasis has been on Christian vocation. One year the committee decided to give people a chance to express themselves. One wall of the exhibit had a large sign at the top— *Ever Want to Say Something?* Underneath were taped several large sheets of blank newsprint, and pens hung ready beside them on strings.

It is an open question how many of the comments were made in the light of the booth's theme and purpose. Quite obviously many were not, for they reflected the questionable standards and taste of any graffiti collection. Some of the contributions are worth pondering, however, inasmuch as they do reflect some general attitudes toward life and because most of them were written by persons under twenty-one years of age.

"Life is death, but with meaning for each and every one of us to decide what it is."
"One day I went down to the sea and caught a fish who looked at me." J. Oregan.
"Teach us to care and not to call
    Teach us to sit still." T.S.E.
"This wall soon to be released in paperback."
"Little me." *Peace.*
"Don't fight for it!
    Work together and achieve it. — Peace."
"We are *puppets* in life."
"I wanna' be free."
"Why are we living?"

"Tomorrow has been cancelled due to lack of interest."
"Today is the tomorrow you thought about yesterday."
"Support LSD. The Fourth network."
"The world is one country and mankind its citizens."
"A man is no fool who gives up what he cannot keep to gain what he cannot lose!"
"What if someone started a war and no one came?"

There are lots of ways of saying things. Not all of our expression of the Christian message is verbal by any means. Not all of our proclamation is on Sunday between eleven and twelve o'clock. Not all of us need to be confined to one or two ultra-restricted vocations as our vehicles of expression. The following pages are dedicated to the opening up of the reader's perspective. If it is possible to present a broader understanding of what ministry can and does mean, if more people are encouraged to venture into new and exciting paths of obedience, if someone else will dare — then this book will have been worthwhile.

The plan of the book allows several approaches to the information required. Chapter 1 lays the groundwork for ministry. The "whys," "hows," and "wherefores" are discussed to set the scene. You will find an analysis of the changing concepts of ministry and an outline of the roots from which our more recent practices have grown. Persons engaged in current practices of ministry are allowed to speak in order that their feelings may be understood and their experiences shared.

Chapter 2 indicates most of the major careers that are open for consideration. Each career carries a very brief outline describing its distinct contribution to ministry and something of the requisites to perform that job.

In chapter 3 the ministries of the local church are described, but even here the outline is greatly expanded to take account of many of the developments on this home front.

Chapter 4 moves outside the walls and seeks to present the opportunities in the dispersed ministries of the church. In chapter 5 experimental ministries are presented with the realization that there is bound to be some overlap with chapter 4. Chapter 5 also deals with the worldwide perspective of Christian service.

Some conclusions follow which again are designed primarily

for those who wish to go beyond the scope of this handbook and to start planning for service in some specific type of ministry.

It is our hope that this handbook will be of use to all persons who are engaged in career counseling — pastors, priests, and youth directors, but primarily persons responsible for guidance in secondary schools, colleges, and universities. The index has been prepared to provide ready reference for those who wish to look up information on specific job opportunities.

If you are looking for a quick guide to the many potential vocations available within Christian ministry, you will want to begin at chapter 2. The various occupational possibilities are listed alphabetically to facilitate identification.

1   "Yes" to Ministry

This book is addressed to those who are primarily responsible for the recruitment of young men and women into some form of Christian ministry. It is written with the hope of providing essential information to those persons who help young people in times of vocational decision. Such persons, we hope, will be encouraged in the performance of their very crucial tasks. It is written with the conviction that a great deal of the vitality and vigor of the church of tomorrow — regardless of its form — is dependent upon the leadership and dedication of its ministry.

The title of this chapter is adapted from a little book[1] written to remind every Christian, young or old, that he is called to some form of Christian service. Many people become lawyers, teachers, doctors, farmers, laborers, and merchants or enter any one of scores of other occupations in which they earn their livelihood. In a very real way a great many of these people look upon their tasks as an avenue of committing themselves to be followers of Jesus Christ. Day by day at their work and in their leisure time activities they seek to become obedient to the claims of God in their lives. In this way they have responded to God's calling (the literal meaning of vocation). Even so, *some are called to church vocations.*

THE CALL TO CHURCH VOCATIONS

Under God's guidance the church must seek out young people

[1] Douglas Webster, *Yes to Mission* (London: SCM Press Ltd, 1966).

whom it sees to be qualified by virtue of their Christian commitment, devotion, talent, and desire and send them out for formal training. It is most often the minister or priest who will sense that a person possesses an aptitude for certain tasks and who sees this as evidence of God's intention for that person's life.

However, we need to realize that many others can play a critical part in this decision-making process. Sometimes the youth counselor, the guidance teacher of the high school, the leader of a camp or conference, or someone else appears as an adult adviser to the person seeking guidance. Not always will it be the minister who is the strongest influence.

We will be looking to these young people whom we seek to influence for the leadership of the churches — in their local congregations or assembly units, in denominational and interdenominational work, in missions at home and overseas, and in scores of other selected labors open to those engaged in ministry today.

There are many ways in which a person may decide to choose a "church vocation." For some, in inexplicable ways the call of God becomes clear to them and they are possessed of a certainty regarding their choice for their life's work. For some persons the call comes as they encounter another person whose deep involvement in his own vocation impresses them with the joy and satisfaction he derives from it. Critical needs arise from time to time, and as these are made known, some people respond. However a person is attracted, once he becomes convinced that this calling is God's will for him, he seeks the ways and means of preparation to obey this "call."

Perhaps at this juncture we need to be very clear and realize that we must not seek to stereotype this experience of a call. Nor is it ever wise to generalize our own limited experience and seek to impose it upon another. This is a temptation to which pastors and priests are peculiarly prone. Sometimes we need to be prepared to accept the impossibility of a reasoned statement and to stand in awe that God in his providence has again acted on his own behalf and that of his church.

For some the realization of a calling grows slowly, almost

imperceptibly. For others this sense of purpose comes as a firm and ringing decision that reorients the life and purpose and that permits no turning back. However it happens, we cannot command or manipulate a call, but we ought to keep open at all times the possibility of its occurrence and be prepared to give proper encouragement in due season. The very sparse record we have of the growing consciousness of the young Jesus is surely very much at point:

> And Jesus increased in wisdom and stature, and in favour with God and man (Luke 2:52, KJV).

and

> Jesus returned in the power of the Spirit into Galilee, and there went out a fame of him through all the region round about. And he taught in their synagogues, being glorified of all (Luke 5:14-15, KJV).

As the young person begins to consider his vocational goals and the matter of full-time Christian vocation comes into direct focus, he will begin to ask some extremely penetrating questions. He is already asking these of himself and will turn to his counselor in order to reflect more deeply upon them. As we have already tried to indicate, for some of these questions there are no hard and fast answers. For others a fairly good body of information is available to us.

SOME TYPICAL QUESTIONS

Does God wish me to serve him in one of these full-time church vocations? Or, to put it more simply and in the form in which it is more likely to occur: *Should I really consider the Christian ministry as my vocation?*

The minister or guidance counselor will need to listen rather carefully if he is to discern the real nature of this question. Not many young people will be able to articulate their intent or true feelings at this point. Some vague but strong feelings are beginning to emerge, and they are looking for someone who can help them to sort out these feelings.

In recent years a new pattern seems to be developing which indicates that this decision is being made at a later chronological stage than before. At one time many young people made their vocational decisions in later elementary school and the bulk of them made such a decision in secondary or high school. Now, in many cases, the decision is postponed until college age and in some instances even later. Seminaries are now discovering a significant number of persons who have worked in the secular sphere for five to fifteen years who have reconsidered their vocational goals and have opted to enter seminary. There they seek to prepare themselves for some form of Christian ministry.

What talents do I possess? Or: *What special skills are required in some of the available Christian vocations?*

At this point the counselee is looking for very specific information about some of the many alternatives open to him. Many of these possibilities are discussed in some detail in chapters 3 and 4. The counselor's general assessment of the young person's potential is, of course, the best starting point. There are some objective tests that he may give, such as those in the check list in the Appendix, but at this stage some trends in vocational choice may become apparent.

The young person may have made a personal decision that he has wrestled out in his own life under the guidance of God. Samuel Southard talks of one divinity student who wrote:

> I do not wish to seem overly pious or spiritual, but I have always been inclined to take all of my problems, or anything that called for a decision, to God. I have received help from personal friends, but I consider this as part of God's directing. Every struggle that I undergo is always in his presence — prayer has been a most vital element in all of my Christian experience.[2]

As the decision begins to take shape in his own mind, the young person is emboldened to share his feelings and intents with someone he trusts. Even here the probes that he puts down may seem rather hesitant and tentative. However, the receptive counselor can provide real support at this stage to enable the person to work out the implications that are developing.

Ideally, of course, at this stage, the person has looked for specific points in his supportive community where he may try out his intentions. In fact, one of the best ways for the pastor to discover the young person's intention in this regard is to observe. For example, one young man was working for the fourth summer as lifeguard at a church-related summer camp.

[2] Samuel Southard, *Counseling for Church Vocations* (Nashville: Broadman Press, 1957), p. 23. Used by permission.

Because it appeared that his interest in teaching the children to swim was unusually attentive, one of the senior counselors, a minister, talked to him about it. The counselor asked him about his background, his family, church, and other interests, and then he inquired whether he had ever considered the Christian ministry as a possible vocation. In this instance it developed that he had not, even though he had been raised in the home of a minister. His vocational goals tended toward medicine, but he was deeply appreciative of the interest shown in him and of the conversations he had shared with the minister concerned.

As the minister observes a young person at work in the church or another agency, he is able to see how much congruence there is between what the person says and how he acts and feels in the company of other persons. For some of these persons there will arise particular questions regarding their involvements with others. Some will sense a need for further training in order to cope with the wide-ranging variety of situations that arise. Some will begin to feel very much more comfortable in working with one age group as compared with another. Some will begin to recognize that the theological issues which emerge are far more basic than they have imagined, and they will be seeking guidance in reading, study, and personal development.

Here we need to be realistic and to recognize that it is at this stage that a perceptive counselor will see incipient evidences of attitudes and personality makeup that may subsequently cause problems. Not everyone is psychologically or otherwise equipped to engage in ministry at the professional level. There will always be the temptation for some persons to seek to do the right things for the wrong reasons. It is becoming the accepted practice for colleges and seminaries to administer tests and to conduct interviews in order to screen out people who are obviously not able to cope with the demands of ministry. In a few instances the high school or college counselor, or minister or priest, may decide that it is not in the best interests of the counselee to pursue a goal of ministry. With tact and care he or she may be able to prevent a disastrous choice. One needs to recognize that in this area it is difficult to formulate and then to interpret a judgment that goes counter to a "call" or a "spiritual vision." However, in the same way in which the shared experiences of the people of God have influenced and molded the church, so we need to rely upon the reasoned and careful judgment of our confidants — even if these judgments sometimes go counter to our own aspirations and cause us to face up to issues that are traumatic and painful. An even more tragic result of our failure to face up to this early in the game is to see a person graduate from both college and seminary and *then* find that he is judged to be unacceptable by his peers. Part of the reason for the rather large dropout rate from the pastoral ministry is to be traced to this point. If more time and more care had been expended by those responsible for admissions to the programs of training, there would be fewer casualties along the way. This judgment is in no way intended as a pejorative comment upon those who have changed their vocational goals for good and sufficient reasons. Nevertheless, there are some persons who could have spent their years of training in more profitable ways both to themselves and to the church.

To what end am I investing my talents? Soren Kierkegaard in *Training in Christianity* makes the distinction between those who are admirers of Christianity and those who are followers of Christ. A direct quotation will make clear the distinction:

> . . . the follower lives in these dangers, while the admirer holds himself aloof from them, though both of them alike acknowledge in words the truth of Christianity. So the distinction holds good nevertheless: the admirer is not willing to make any sacrifices, to give up anything worldly, to reconstruct his life, to be what he admires or let his life express it — but in words, verbal expressions, . . . he is inexhaustible in affirming how highly he prizes Christianity. The follower, on the other hand, aspires to be what he admires — and so . . . even though he lives in established Christendom he will encounter the same danger which once was involved in confessing Christ. . . .
>
> But yet the admirer is in the strictest sense no true Christian, only the follower is such.[3]

As a person seriously contemplates the question of ministry, he is almost overwhelmed by both the timorous quality of his aspiration and the scope of the task. He wonders very seriously

---

[3] Soren Kierkegaard, *Training in Christianity*, trans. Walter Lowrie (Princeton, N. J.: Princeton University Press, 1941), pp. 245, 249.

whether his little contribution can ever make any significant difference in the state of the word. He is tempted to deprecate his own talents and capacities to function as a change-agent in the pluralistic society of our day. These are not new reactions or feelings. From the very outset men have stood trembling before the call of God to assume obedient leadership. Moses was a most reluctant leader of his people. As he stood before the bush that burned but was not consumed and heard the voice of the Lord, he replied: "Who am I that I should go to Pharaoh, and bring the sons of Israel out of Egypt?" (Exodus 3:11). Here a most interesting exchange is recorded as the voice of God reasoned with Moses and promised him that as he took upon himself the responsibility of confronting Pharaoh, God would be with him to strengthen and enable him. Moses still had his doubts. "But behold, they will not believe me or listen to my voice, for they will say, 'The Lord did not appear to you'" (Exodus 4:1). Moses then was commanded to throw the rod in his hand to the ground so it might become a serpent. When he took it up, it was restored to a rod. This and other demonstrations of the power behind the call of the Lord finally convinced Moses that the power would be God's and not Moses', and Moses went out to do as he had been bidden.

Many biblical illustrations of this phenomenon could be introduced here to underline this point. Space does not permit us to speak of Gideon, Jonah, Jeremiah, Saul/Paul, and even some of the disciples. Yet in each case when the conviction came and obedience resulted, the power to minister in God's name brought remarkable results.

A recent document entitled *Essays in Ministry* contains material that has been gathered by The Fund for Theological Education, Inc. This organization has sponsored men in a trial year of seminary education. The purpose is to help men who have been enrolled in other disciplines to discover whether they are interested in pursuing a complete theological education leading to some form of ministry. Several comments from these *Essays in Ministry* will help us to see how some persons have sought to come to grips with our question.

It was on the level of action that my call came to the ministry. Perhaps it was one of those negative calls — but no less vigorous. It came in the collapse of my father at an early age largely due to overwork and all the result of small men in high places. One gets bitter against the church and will have no more to do with it; or one catches oneself asking why the Church is always addressed in the third person — those people over there! When one realizes that the Church involves him, then comes the push toward giving something better to the Church than it has presently. I must admit that this is a call which has always been with me in every change. . . . never a desire to advance, I don't know what that is, but always a call like that which came over the telephone from my predecessor here at Cambridge when I had already decided that I was going to fight my way through the problems of a Southern parish, "But Henry, you should see the names of the Joes that they are suggesting for this place." That has always been enough for me.[4]

What an assortment for one man . . . and in every case the call to new endeavour was not sought . . . . the need sought me out . . . . in every case there was a tense situation — a broader situation into which to move . . . . in every case new efforts were met with opposition and no one knew what I was doing at the time . . . . in every case the strangest kinds of fruits have attended the work — often the seeds which were scattered in the most barren areas were the ones that came up. My faith in the Holy Spirit is firm — but the evidence is always in *retro*spect, not in *pro*spect![5]

I feel a kinship to the middle class people I serve. I can feel with them and share with them and have fun with them. I know their guilt, because it is mine. I know their possibilities, because they are mine. I am glad to be where I am, because there is much to do.[6]

The person committed to ministry thinks of himself as allied with God in the most important labor to which he can respond. One writer has summed it up in this way:

Yet I see the local minister as one of those fellows who, if he will work at the job, can persuade, can effect changes, can bring about a real difference in the climate. A minister is able, just because he is a minister, to talk with almost anyone in the community. He can approach people with openness and a desire to be helpful. We should not discount this role. Granted there are limitations as to what we can accomplish, but the role of conciliator is still one of the instruments made available to us.[7]

[4] *Essays in Ministry* (Princeton, N. J.: The Fund for Theological Education, n.d.), p. 25.
[5] *Ibid*, p. 26.
[6] *Ibid*, p. 140.
[7] Robert G. Kemper, "Emerson Colaw: Man in the Middle, An Interview," *The Christian Ministry*, May, 1970, p. 54. Reprinted by permission.

Christians have always been aware that when their lives are caught up in the purposes of God and the true destinies of men, they are most truly blessed. They become aware of God's acting in the world on his own behalf and in behalf of that world. Christians look toward the fulfillment of that work and toward the establishment of that day when God's kingdom shall be realized. In the meantime they are willing to endure the necessary hardships, toils, and burdens of obedience knowing that their faithful labors will find blessing.

CHANGING PERSPECTIVES

The process of self-evaluation is a difficult but necessary part of every profession. The profession or occupation is rare, indeed, in which its practitioners are not bringing under careful scrutiny all that they do. One important aspect of this self-study is to look at other professionals to see how they function, how they view their work in relation to other professions, and how a team approach to the issues and problems within a community can work to the betterment of all concerned.

The various forms of ministry available to a person today have a direct relationship to the so-called "helping professions" with which they must be yoked. No longer is the pastor or priest of the local church the "norm" of ministry. Indeed, every time a new opportunity for a diversified form of ministry has developed, there has been the necessity for reevaluation. Also, the type of commitment to these varying ministries has also undergone changes. More churches, agencies, and organizations than ever before now offer "short-term" openings to qualified persons to become involved in a particular aspect of their outreach. These openings are kept under evaluation and may or may not be renewed depending upon the changing situations as they develop. An agency may not accomplish what was envisaged and therefore is unwilling to renew the contract. It may be, also, that the employee is dissatisfied with the developing conditions and is ready to move out to another sphere of work. In either case, there is no prejudice or negative judgment brought against the persons involved. Those who are considering such work, however, need to have these prospects in mind.

In addition to this situation, there are many persons who are interested in and willing to make a commitment to some form of ministry for a definite period, five, seven, or ten years, maybe even a shorter time, before settling into a so-called secular profession which may become their vocation. The average employee in the work force in North America makes several job changes in the thirty-five to forty years of his working life; so this attitude is a true reflection of a developing pattern. This practice is, of course, parallel to the concept of short-term service that has come through Peace Corps, VISTA, and other agencies in which volunteer participation for a limited term of service has been enlisted.

A person trained in a discipline other than theology finds it easier to make this kind of decision than someone with professional theological education. If a person invests six or seven years of his life in getting a theological education, he will be more inclined to choose forms of ministry that promise longer periods of meaningful service than three to five years. Even here one cannot generalize. Some people find that their theological education is quite portable and can be useful in alternate positions of ministry. Some of these positions, such as counseling, are quite closely parallel to the more traditional ministries; others, such as probation work, juvenile and family court work, or social service, are quite dissimilar. The prospect is that more young people will be looking to seminaries and theological colleges for a year or two of theological education to provide a working basis for their vocation and to allow them to function in non-ordained roles, maybe as para-theological personnel (similar to para-medical) in a wide variety of situations.

In the next chapter we will consider some specific opportunities for ministry. The young person reading these descriptions will also wish to ponder these two Scripture verses and the following Check List.

And Jesus increased in wisdom and stature, and in favour with God and man (Luke 2:52, KJV).

And Jesus returned in the power of the Spirit into Galilee, and there went out a fame of him through all the region round about. And he taught in their synagogues, being glorified of all (Luke 4:14-15, KJV).

CHECK LIST

1. Keep your mind and heart open to God's continued guidance.
2. Keep yourself informed. Get the facts about career opportunities. Keep abreast of the training requirements.
3. Take interest, aptitude, and intelligence tests.
4. Try to deepen your understanding of yourself.
5. Read widely about church vocations.
6. Plan to get the most from your education. The best colleges and schools will be glad to send you catalogs and information.
7. Attend conferences when possible. Here you will meet others who are seeking for guidance and those who can provide the help you need.
8. Deepen your own spiritual life.
9. Guard your physical and emotional health.
10. Keep in touch with your minister and denominational leaders who can guide you.

2

No Limit

"Your life is without a foundation if,
in any matter, you choose on your own behalf."
Dag Hammarskjold, 1953 [1]

The possibilities open to someone contemplating ministry are endless. Of course, the traditional avenues of pastoral service and missionary service are open, but even in these areas a great many variations are being introduced. Perhaps a bare listing of many of the possible church vocations, with a word or two of explanation, will help to further the process of selection. A more inclusive discussion of some of these vocations will be found in later chapters.

ACCOUNTANT — Many agencies and churches require the services of people trained in accountancy and the use of computers. Larger congregations are hiring business managers who administer the entire financial structure of the church. In many instances the total budget and staff of these church agencies is very large, at least equal to that of many small businesses.

AGRICULTURALIST — There are openings both on the North American continent and abroad for persons skilled in agriculture. Some of the positions are short-term for a year or two while others are projected over many years. Listings of these positions are readily available from denominational offices and national councils of churches.

---

[1] Dag Hammarskjold, *Markings*, trans. Leif Sjoberg and W. H. Auden (New York: Alfred A. Knopf, Inc., 1964), p. 93.

ARTISTS — the publication of books, curriculum materials, magazines, and papers is a vital aspect of religious education. All major agencies require persons with artistic skills to produce literature. A great percentage of this material is produced cooperatively, and the processes are centralized for reasons of economy and efficiency.

BOOKSTORE MANAGER — In many large population centers there are bookstores where books and literature related to religion may be purchased. Again, many of these are cooperative ventures sponsored by agencies or federations of churches and denominations. Literature for Christian education in church schools, camps, vacation schools, and lay training projects are all stocked in these stores.

CONGREGATIONAL WORKER — A number of titles are used to designate people who hold full-time positions in team ministries alongside and in cooperation with ordained clergy. Some of the titles are parish worker, deaconess, pastor's assistant, director of Christian education, youth worker, and project coordinator. Many of these persons have formal theological training; others utilize skills acquired in other ways. Some are ordained while others function as lay persons.

CHAPLAIN — A wide variety of openings in chaplaincy service is available to qualified applicants. There are roughly three main groups of chaplains:

Hospital — Most large hospitals now have a regularly established chaplaincy office which provides an ecumenical service for their patients. The chaplain is available as a part of the healing team to counsel, visit, conduct services, administer the sacraments, and generally minister to the sick and distressed. He will, of course, be concerned to provide services for the families of those who are in the hospital or receiving treatment. In cases where only one chaplain is a full-time employee on the staff of a hospital, arrangements are made to have representatives of other communions or religions on call to be ready as requested by patients or their families.

Hospital chaplains are appointed in various ways, some on recommendation of denominational committees, some by interfaith committees, some by direct action (usually in consultation with the religious community) of the institution administrator. In almost all cases a basic degree from a recognized college or university plus an accepted theological degree plus ordination in the chaplain's denomination are required of the applicants. It is becoming almost universally accepted that a chaplain shall have received training in Clinical Pastoral Training or Supervised Pastoral Education (both terms are used). If a chaplain has been licensed by the American (or Canadian) Council for Supervised Pastoral Education, he is able to train students within his institution and he becomes a Chaplain Supervisor. A percentage of these chaplains also take further training as counselors and receive certification from the American (Canadian) Association of Pastoral Counselors.

Military — The armed forces appoint certain persons who have been recommended by their denominational and/or interdenominational boards to chaplaincy positions. These positions are worked out on a percentage basis to enable the chaplains to provide pastoral care to a certain number of personnel and their families. In almost every instance the chaplain functions without any direct reference to a denomination; he is merely designated as Protestant, Roman Catholic, or Jewish.

The duties of the chaplain are roughly equivalent to those of a parish minister or priest except that his parishioners are probably much more mobile.

Institutional — This classification is intended to include all kinds of chaplaincy services which may be provided to correctional institutions, jails, reformatories, detention centers, and the courts. In addition to the qualifications recommended for chaplains of hospitals, the chaplain of a reform institution must have training in the legal implications of his work. He will be expected to understand the kind of prison term that has been meted out to a person and why; he will need to be aware of the possibilities of parole and various kinds of treatment facilities that may be open to the offender. He will, of course, be called upon to keep open the limited channels of communication between the world of the prison and the outside world, hopefully to assist in the return of the prisoner to society and to a useful life. The shocks that are involved to everyone connected with such imprisonment are very great and the chaplain is called upon at least to give support, if not to lessen the shocks of transition.

Again, the chaplain must serve in the prison or penitentiary situation in concert with many other people. He needs to have a keen awareness of his role and that of others who function alongside him.

COUNSELOR — In recent years the role of pastoral counselor as a specialized form of ministry has developed. There have always been people in the pastoral office who have served as counselors and confidants, but now this has become a specialty.

In many cases the counselor functions as a part of the team ministry of a local church or a federation of churches. People who have need of counseling are referred to him by other pastors and persons who are aware of his skills and availability. Some of these people serve in the setting of a Pastoral Counseling Agency or Institute which may function as an independent unit or in concert with a church or churches.

The person who is contemplating a period of service in pastoral counseling will need the same basic qualifications as a chaplain: a basic arts or science degree, a theological degree from an approved seminary or college, and ordination according to his denominational practice. In addition to clinical pastoral education[2] he will need to be approved by the American Association of Pastoral Counselors. A list of their requirements is readily available to all interested persons.

CHRISTIAN EDUCATION DIRECTOR — The staff of many local congregations provides a place for a specialist in Christian education. The person may be ordained or a lay person and he

[2] Further information on clinical pastoral training can be obtained from the Council for Clinical Training, 475 Riverside Drive, N.Y.C.; The Institute of Pastoral Care, P.O. Box 57, Worcester, Mass.; or the Canadian Council for Supervised Pastoral Education in Canada, Box 2532, London, Ontario.

usually functions as an integral part of the team ministry. This job responsibility focuses attention upon the importance of the teaching ministry of the church. In company with other persons working in a multiple-staff church, the minister or director of Christian education has his or her prime responsibility in the teaching ministry of the church. The main requirements are for the supervision, coordination, and the continuing life of the congregation as it seeks to become more involved in the teaching ministry of the Christian church. Probably the key role of the director will be that of leadership development. Adequate leaders need to be discovered, recruited, trained, and then supervised in their work. The director may employ many methods of training, such as preservice training; periodic training opportunities, such as workshops and clinics; and in-service training. Library and curriculum materials are made available as required. All of these and many more resources are planned to help the willing person to become a more effective teacher or leader in Christian education.

Special seminary programs leading to the Bachelor and Master of Religious Education degrees are available for potential directors of religious education. These programs normally follow the completion of a B.A. degree program and require two years for their completion.

Many city societies or state councils of churches employ specialists in Christian education, and there are a variety of employment possibilities open in overseas mission agencies. Such lists are available through denominational head offices.

DIRECTORS OF CHRISTIAN CENTERS — As the local congregation seeks to move "outside the walls," various centers are being established alongside the church buildings, in quite distant places, in inner-city storefront locations, and in apartments. Some of these are drop-in centers for youth; some are distress centers to assist people experiencing difficulties because of urban blight, alcoholism, drug-addiction or delinquency. Others merely seek to reach a cross section of a given population. Many skills are required in these centers, depending upon the aims and purposes that have been laid down. In most of them a large percentage of the personnel is made up of volunteers who work in close liaison with the professional staff.

DOCTOR — The variety of medical skills needed by various church agencies for service in America and abroad is endless. The needs of one world-famous institution illustrate the expectations for medical personnel:

> Doctors, aged 45-60, men and women needed for teaching at university level as well as hospital practice. Should have appropriate degree standing, at least two years of experience and teaching. Current needs are:
> Pharmacist — hospital and business experience
> Physiologist — man or woman
> Ophthalmologist, man or woman
> Obstetrician and Gynecologist
> Diagnostic Radiologist
> Teacher of Anatomy, M.D. or Ph.D. (6 years experience to teach in medical college)
> Pathologist
> Anaesthesiologist, preferable regular term
> Cardiologist, Sr. man or woman, professor grade. Regular term.
> 2 Radiologists, 1 Diagnostic, 1 Therapy, experienced in work and teaching.
> Senior Obstetrician-Gynecologist, man or woman with FRCS [or equivalent] — teaching experience necessary.
> 2 Physicians, with specialty, preferably teaching experience.[3]

EDITOR-WRITER — For persons with skills in communications there are many opportunities in denominational, church-related, and independent organizations connected with publications. The type of occupation ranges from the editorship of daily, weekly, or monthly denominational journals to the production of publicity and promotional materials for local camp committees.

As stated above under *Artist,* such publications provide a vital contribution in religious education.

A good grounding in a person's basic working language is a prime requisite with a degree from an accredited university or college. Various schools of journalism and writing offer specialty courses beyond the B.A. level. Of course it is frequently advantageous to have a working knowledge of a second language.

[3] *Jobs Worth Doing,* 1969. (Toronto: Canadian Council of Churches), p. 2.

EVANGELIST — The work of evangelism takes many forms ranging from the simplest one-to-one approach to the very highly organized mass evangelism approaches. There are "outreach" programs not categorized as evangelism which are designed with the one objective of the proclamation of the gospel. Most major denominations have an office of evangelism either separate or as a part of a unified approach, e.g., social service and evangelism. In any case, people are employed full time as field representatives, promotion secretaries, organizers, and preachers.

For most forms of evangelism a complete theological education is recommended, to be followed by whatever apprenticeship or specialized training the sponsoring agency may require. It should be kept in mind that many people look upon evangelism as the very *raison d'être* of the individual church or Christian. Therefore the only real purpose of an evangelist or a department of evangelism is to make it possible for people to become more effective evangelists in themselves. Thus, the professional evangelist or staff uses more a training and enabling approach than direct practice. The real locus of evangelism has always been the local congregation of believers. Boards and departments of evangelism frequently *do* employ persons who go about preaching, teaching, and doing the work of evangelism. For the most part, however, these boards are more concerned to provide the impetus and the methods of evangelism to local congregations so that they themselves become evangelists. Schools of evangelism are conducted; materials and encouragement are provided. The methods of evangelism — personal, visitation, mass, radio-TV, etc. — all of these are coordinated in the "outreach" program at the local level.

EXECUTIVE — Interdenominational — Denominational — YMCA–YWCA — etc. Each major clustering of churches, be they denominational or ecumenical groupings, employs one or more executive secretaries. The function performed by such persons includes the day-to-day administration of the organization concerned, the personnel matters related to senior staff, the relationships that exist between the various sectors of the organization's life, and, of course, the public relations with the constituency and the community at large. It is probable that the funding of the organization will be of central concern to the executive secretary who will bear ultimate responsibility for the program to be underwritten and for the manner in which monies are expended.

The wider relationships that exist between denominational bodies and groupings are usually facilitated and encouraged by the executive offices of the bodies concerned. This relationship encourages cooperation at many levels and in widely diversified sections of the globe and thus is a very important part of the secretarial office.

HOME ECONOMIST — The skills of a home economist are in demand among agencies which work in areas of underprivilege or privation. In some rural as well as urban areas people need assistance with matters of nutrition, homemaking, health practices, and budgeting. All of these may be provided by an agency seeking to develop a total approach to the needs of an area or a grouping of people.

Wherever there are schools and colleges under denominational or mission auspices, the teaching of home economics is a vital part of the curriculum.

LINGUIST — As our world shrinks in size and we live in a "global village," it becomes more important that we be able to translate other languages into our own and ours into others. Religious news services are constantly seeking persons with linguistic skills.

Another area of service open to those with language facility is in the training of missionaries and others to serve abroad. Those who intend to work in other countries need to be able at least to converse in a second language if their work is to be effective. The matter of facilitating the entry of immigrants into North America calls for persons who are bi- or multilingual to help in the period of transition and settlement.

Further translation of Scriptures and other religious material is still needed, and many people find useful service as translators. The Wycliffe Bible Translators are an excellent example of this form of ministry.

MUSICIAN — One of the most applicable talents that can develop is that of music. It is a rare congregation that does not hire at least some one person to give direction to the musical portion of its program. Ministers of music, directors of choirs, organists, and soloists all are able to contribute their services either part or full time. Some very large churches, such as Riverside, New York City, even employ a full-time carillonneur. The wide ranging application of musical skills to other than worship occasions in the life of the church is perhaps even more important. Youth meetings, drop-in centers, camps, informal occasions of many kinds — all of these are natural settings for the exercise of the ministry of music. If musical abilities can be combined with other talents, so much the better. Music will sometimes open doors that otherwise might remain closed.

It is impossible or unnecessary to list the kinds of training needed for a career in music. Suffice it to say, the better prepared one is, the better he is able to utilize his talents and further his ultimate purpose of service.

NURSE — Perhaps one of the most portable skills one can possess is that of nursing. The routes to qualification are varied and one needs to have as clear an idea as to ultimate goals as possible, a question more easily stated than accomplished. To be more specific, if one is ultimately interested in public health work or nursing education, one probably ought to pursue a university degree program comparable to a B.Sc.N. course. In some sections of the continent it is possible to proceed beyond the more usual registered nurse program and to develop specialties.

Most nurses who desire to function under Christian auspices both on this continent and overseas will find themselves in relatively isolated sections of the country. This means that the resident nurse must fill many roles other than that of traditional "bedside nursing," such as midwifery, dental education, and even general medicine. On every continent there is an emphasis on public health. In recent years the developing countries have been requesting people to train indigenous leadership and to conduct training programs at many levels. Obviously experience in the homeland is necessary before service overseas. It is not overly dramatic to state that in some areas the time limits for missionary personnel are quite short so that the time remaining must be used in the development of a self-sustaining entity (be it a health-care program or some other) to be left behind. Conditions, of course, vary greatly from country to country. Persons working in the area of medicine enjoy a high degree of acceptance and are among the last to be excluded when restrictions are imposed.

OFFICE PERSONNEL — This is rather a catch-all category that includes many positions open to persons with business training and interests. It is obvious that the needs of each organization will vary with its size and purpose, but most large denominational and interdenominational agencies will employ persons filling the usual office categories.

ORDAINED MINISTER — For the immediate, foreseeable future it is likely that the ordained minister will continue to be the backbone of the church's ministry. More attention will be given to this office in a later chapter. Suffice it to say at this point that the requisites in the major denominations and communions are graduation from college or university with a baccalaureate degree, a full seminary course leading to the B.D., M.Div., S.T.M., or D.Min. degrees, and, in some cases a year of service in a parish situation leading to ordination. In some communions ordination procedures are closely linked with the training programs provided; in other instances they are quite separate. It ought to be noted here that ordination does not necessarily mean that the person will be a "priest," "pastor," "minister," or "preacher." It means that the community of faith is accepting the person for service as an ordained clergyman and is setting him apart to perform that ministry. He or she may serve in the traditional sense as the minister or priest of the local congregation, or as a pastoral visitor, a counselor, a community worker, a missioner, or whatever. Any or all of these persons may be ordained clergy although their duties may not reflect the expectations that the term "Reverend" has connoted for many in the church across the years.

PROFESSOR — Every communion and denomination maintains colleges and seminaries for the training of its youth. In spite of the fact that direct control of some of these institutions is passing out of the hands of the church, there are still many openings for teachers and professors. The largest number of opportunities exist in the developing countries of the world where North Americans are needed to serve as specialists and consultants for short-term positions. One recent bulletin read:

> Graduates are urgently needed for the staffs of Asian Christian Colleges of university level. Men and women who hold (or expect to hold) honours degrees first or second class in the subject to be taught, who are Christians and are prepared to go out for three years are invited. . . .[4]

Some of the categories listed are: Dairy Engineer, Chemistry, Natural Sciences, English, Philosophy, and Political Science.

Those who have a particular interest in seminary teaching ought to realize that it is a very limited field. Fewer, albeit larger, seminaries, are engaged in theological education and the number of openings is decidedly limited. Many seminaries look to persons with a wide background in the life of the church who also have skills and developed competencies in one area of specialization. For many people seminary teaching became possible as an alternate opportunity; they had not set their minds upon it as a primary goal. In almost every case, persons expecting to teach at the seminary level should hold a Ph.D. or its equivalent.

PROGRAM WORKER — In addition to the YMCA and YWCA there are numerous other organizations which use program staff as the bulwark of their work. The needs of these organizations may be readily ascertained. Though they vary from year to year, you will certainly find openings for the following:[5]

> General group program directors and assistants
> Health and physical education directors and assistants
> Counsellors
> Residence directors
> Camp directors and senior staff

In the overseas programs:

> Advisory Secretary
> Bilingual program staff to work with YMCA-YWCA

[4] *Jobs Worth Doing*, 1969, p. 3.   [5] *Jobs Worth Doing*, 1969, p. 5.

Baby clinics, Cottage industries
Staff consultants

The YWCA puts its needs this way:

— Basic academic qualification is university graduation with appropriate specialization: adult education, health and physical education, recreation, religious education or social work.

— Wanted are young women with initiative and imagination, an understanding and acceptance of people of varying backgrounds, interest and concern for social issues, good health, and motivated to work in a world organization with a Christian purpose.

The YMCA says it this way:

We are looking for people who have, or will have, their college degree. We would like some of the courses to be in the social science area. We seek persons who want to work with people in a voluntary private organization, such as the YMCA. We want them to be in good health. Most important, we seek a person who is motivated by Christian beliefs and who wants to work in an organization with the same kind of purpose.[6]

Much of the work that is being carried on in the inner city is of a program type. Workers are needed to man community centers, to conduct day care centers, nurseries, tutoring programs, "Head Start" programs, and camping programs.

RESIDENCE DIRECTOR — On many campuses church bodies maintain residences for students which are operated by residence directors and staff. These residences offer accommodation but may also provide a variety of services to the residents. Some private schools at the primary and secondary school level offer residential accommodation to young people who for various reasons prefer to take their education outside the public sector.

Residence directors and "dons" are employed to operate such residences.

In the overseas program of the church there are many openings for this type of work. In some instances teachers combine their work with residence life and offer guidance to their students at both levels of school life. The role of the resident is particularly important where advanced schooling is less plentiful and where the students need to travel considerable distances to complete their education.

[6] *Ibid.*, pp. 5-6.

SEXTON — One of the least heralded and yet most important occupations within the local church is that of the sexton. If he is functioning properly, his work goes unnoticed. The building is well maintained, is opened and closed as required; the boards, committees, and organizations are properly housed. All of this happens if the sexton (caretaker, custodian, janitor, superintendent, or whatever) is performing adequately. It goes without saying, yet is often forgotten, that the caretaker or sexton needs to have a congenial manner if he is to cope with the many people who will call upon him for service.

Basic Christian commitment to the aims and purposes of the organization is essential; beyond that the formal requirements for the job are not very great.

TEACHER — Much of what was said above under the category of *Professor* also applies here. Many denominations and communions operate schools and colleges at all levels of education. Most of these institutions are subject to the rules and regulations which govern education in the state or province where they are located; so their teacher requirements parallel those in the public school systems. It is wise for the prospective teacher to read the statutes in advance of his training period.

By far the most pressing demands for teachers come from countries outside the North American continent. High school teachers are required in all of the developing countries, including Colombia, Congo, Egypt, Hong Kong, India, and Japan.

More and more interest is developing among prospective teachers in short-term appointments which run from two to three years. To give but one example, the Overseas Appointment Bureau was established in 1952 to help independent Christian schools recruit suitable teachers:

> The Bureau recruits Christian teachers who are graduates for church-related schools in Africa, the West Indies, Hong Kong. Teaching certificates or experience essential. Recommendation usually follows interview. Usual contract for two or three years with travel paid and high salary rates.[7]

[7] *Jobs Worth Doing*, 1969, p. 3.

An up-to-date listing of the positions open for such teaching opportunities is available from the Canadian Council of Churches or the National Council of Churches and/or from the head offices of the major denominations. Because of the rapid changes in these listings it is not possible to be more specific about these possibilities at this point.

Summer service opportunities in teaching are also available through the Frontier College in Canada and should be explored by those who would like to experiment in order to find out their capacities in this regard. For primary education, graduation from high school or junior college plus one or two years of teachers' college training is the minimum preparation one ought to consider. For secondary education a degree from an accredited university or college with a developed speciality is recommended. These range from English and physical education to Spanish, Russian, etc. Other assignments not as closely related to classroom teaching are also available. These include guidance and counseling services, library science, remedial reading, psychologists, and curriculum development people.

SOCIAL WORKER — The disciplines of social work are being drawn upon by many church-related agencies in their attempts to broaden their ministries to the community. In inner-city situations where the needs of the community are diverse and multidimensional; in areas where subcultures such as the "drug" and "hippie" cultures need ministry; in the suburban areas of high alienation and family crisis situations; in all of these and many more places, the skills of social workers are being utilized.

Frequently the church or its related agencies are calling upon other helping professions as consultants or as places of referral. It is becoming even more common for social workers to be a part of the church agency staff and to function as an integral part of the team.

The requirements for social work include a university course in the social sciences followed by a bachelor's or master's degree in social work. In many cases social workers prefer to specialize in certain areas, and so pursue courses of study to enhance their skills at these points.

TV — COMMUNICATIONS — AUDIO-VISUALS — A very large field of employment is developing in relation to multi-media for use by churches and church-related agencies. Educational specialists, communication resource centers, and production staffs are required to provide materials adequate for today's cultural scene.

Wherever people are desirous of telling a story or transmitting a message, there will be the need for media. The writing of material, the production of concepts, layouts and form, the arting of the concepts, the production into tapes, records, filmstrips, movies or still pictures — all of these steps require skilled staff.

Because of the tremendous variety of occupational skills which can be utilized in the field, it is impossible to specify training requirements. Special courses in the communication arts are available from the post-secondary school level through advanced graduate studies.

One factor that needs to be kept in mind at this point is that many people are utilizing the newer or modern media in conjunction with other disciplines. This means that they are taking summer courses, extension course offerings, workshops, and the like, in an attempt to master at least the rudiments of communication theory. An awareness of the basics enables such persons to "feed in" their skills in order to complement the genius of the media. This preparation facilitates planning, writing, and utilization and insures a better end product for all concerned.

URBAN STUDIES — Research Analysts — Community Development People — Since the largest percentage of our population lives in cities, we need to develop an awareness of the characteristics of urban life. Departments of urban research have been developed denominationally and cooperatively to strengthen the work of the ministry within cities. Sometimes the services of persons skilled in urban ecology are employed on a consultative basis; at other times such people are made a part of a permanent staff.

The understandings that come from the social sciences, particularly sociology and geography, are basic requisites for anyone desiring employment in this area. There are also centers of urban training where persons learn the dynamics of the city and develop methods of influencing the decision-making processes and the political structures of the city. The Ecumenical Institute, The Urban Training Center in Chicago, The Center for Urban Training in Toronto, and the Metropolitan Urban Service Training (MUST) in New York City are all examples of places where people interested in deepening their understanding of the dynamics of urban life may go for training.

WRITER — The category of Editor–Writer discussed earlier covers this area.

SUMMER SERVICE VOLUNTEER — As with other forms of volunteer service, the volunteers are usually young persons who are encouraged to view their term of service as much an opportunity for learning as it is to bring objective value to the project, the community, or the country being served. Some of the projects which have been organized, most of which last for two consecutive months, are to organize professional services for "hippy communities," to provide recreational activities for various age groups, or to work with North American Indian communities.

It is reasonable to expect that the participant's expenses will be covered by the sponsoring agency, and in many cases the group members are required to attend a week-long training session before embarking on the project. This training familiarizes each member with the goals of the agency and the particular project and allows sufficient interaction among group members to facilitate cooperative action. In most cases the experience is evaluated at the end of the summer.

Ecumenical work camps are a summer opportunity in which a carefully selected group of fifteen to twenty Christian youth is chosen representing both international and ecumenical backgrounds. These people are volunteers who take a vacation period (3-4 weeks) and spend it in work and service.

One set of specifications reads:

Applicants should be:
— between 19 and 30 years of age;
— able and willing to do simple, but often strenuous work;

— ready to adapt to unfamiliar and sometimes difficult conditions of camp life;

— able to speak at least one of the languages of the camp.[8]

Anyone interested in spending a summer of service similar to those described above should contact the National Council of Churches, the Canadian Council of Churches, or their denominational headquarters for up-to-date information. The openings vary from year to year according to demands and needs. It is unwise to assume that particular projects will continue from year to year.

SUMMER SERVICE — EMPLOYMENT — At present there are fewer summer service opportunities available for which the young person receives remuneration. Some of these are in camping programs, recreation, mission field situations, etc. Again, it is wise to contact the agencies mentioned above for specific information.

[8] *Jobs Worth Doing,* 1969, p. 5.

3   Ministries on Location

"How humble the tool when praised
for what the hand has done."
Dag Hammarskjold [1]

By now, it should be clear that ministry is no longer of one type, that the concept of THE MINISTER is long since outmoded. Persons are needed who are able to see life whole, who will be theologically trained, who will be able to develop skills to help people to influence their total environment not only within the church but also through the church.

MINISTRIES ON LOCATION

This chapter will be devoted to a consideration of those ministries which we have traditionally associated with the local church. We will take notice of the changes both in style and variety within these ministries and will try to spell out something of the distinctiveness which each of them possesses.

Perhaps we need to be explicit about something that has not been specifically mentioned before. The "role" of minister or the "function" of ministry does not in any way connote a "maleness" about these vocations. Each Christian, man or woman, is called to ministry. As the church reassesses its total tasks, women will have the opportunity to move into significant positions of leadership at all levels of life. Already, there is a highly developed corps of women who are "manning" coffee houses and friendship centers, and who are providing excellent liaison between the local church and community resources. There are many women

[1] Dag Hammarskjold, *Markings*, trans. Leif Sjoberg and W. H. Auden (New York: Alfred A. Knopf, Inc., 1964), p. 140.

who have received full professional training and who are serving in a number of different ways, as ministers in local churches and in denominational service.

Christian vocations, short term, long term, and as avocations, are opening which compel the interests and loyalty of women of all ages. If the tasks are sufficiently challenging, the time and the talent will be forthcoming.

We have long since moved out of the days when the men who exercised ministry and those to whom they ministered knew precisely what that ministry was. H. Richard Niebuhr quoted Professor Mark A. May in *The Purpose of the Church and Its Ministry* as he wrestled with the problems of stating precisely what the ministry is:

> Entering the ministry is more like entering the army, where one never knows where he will land or live or what specific work he will be called upon to perform. This lack of clear definition of the functions of the pastor that can be widely accepted influences theological education. . . . How can the seminaries train men for a work that is so tenuous, and concerning the nature of which such a diversity of opinion exists? [2]

We may define ministry as that which leads men and women in response to the call of God into some form of *edifying* the church, of enabling the people of God to serve the world more effectively so that there will result an increase among men of love for God and neighbor. The people of the church and the minister alike are ministers, and the "minister" as the professional leader (Pastoral Director is another fruitful title that has been suggested[3]) exercises his gifts in order to make the people more effective in their calling.

For the foreseeable future, however, in spite of the problems of definition and description, there are many who feel that the local congregation of believers, by whatever name it is called, will continue to be at the heart of the church. It is self-evident that the local manifestation of the church must and will change. It is equally certain that not all of the pressures for change are coming from the outside. A healthy discontent is building which

[2] H. Richard Niebuhr, *The Purpose of the Church and Its Ministry* (New York: Harper & Row, Publishers, 1956), pp. 51-52.

[3] See *ibid.*, pp. 79-94.

makes it possible for members of the local congregation to grapple in the most exciting ways with their role, their responsibilities, and their opportunities for ministry in their locale.

One congregation in a metropolitan area of Ontario established a committee of its members to engage in long-term planning. They were empowered to explore every facet of the congregation's life and existence. Out of a long and honored tradition, with a distinguished service from both ministers and congregation behind them, these people sought to look forward to an even greater future of ministry. Two paragraphs out of a statement made as a report to the congregation indicate how deeply the commitment of the people is rooted:

> We have been a very effective congregation in the past and we have a very strong tradition. It is true that many of our organizations are weak and some are ineffective. Nevertheless many individual members of the congregation are providing very valuable service in the community. In other words we have a lot of strength and a lot of talent to call on if we choose to make use of it.
>
> There is a great deal of changing around us and we must change with the times. There is a new emphasis on leisure activities. There is rebellion among young people manifested not only in the challenge to authority but in the growing use of drugs and alcohol. There is a groping for a more meaningful life which underlies this rebellion. In all this the church seems less involved than it used to be.

This committee went on to direct the membership of the congregation in a consideration of the services of worship, the role and future of the constituent organizations of the church, its membership strengths, the type of ministry now in effect, and the kinds of ministry that ought to emerge. It looked at the ministry to transients, the inner core of the city, youth work, social services, new facilities, and the relationship of the church to the university.

This congregation is cited as a not-too-typical illustration of the developments that are emerging in many places. The minister of the local church must work within such a setting. If the environment of his congregation is not as friendly as he would like, he has the responsibility and opportunity to seek for change. Sometimes the process will seem painfully slow and he may be tempted to succumb to discouragement.

To extend their ministry the members of Central Baptist Church, of Wayne, Pennsylvania, voted to assume a mortgage on their own church building in order to raise $100,000 as a trust fund to be called the Martin Luther King Memorial Fund.[4]

As this congregation assessed the social, political, and especially black-white issues of the United States, it became aware of its own responsibility. Ten trustees were elected to administer the fund and to recommend the projects which would receive congregational aid.

One hundred thousand dollars was raised, and in nine months all of the monies had been allocated. More than ten thousand dollars went to a program dedicated to helping individuals develop skills they could use in industry. Housing for low-income families was another project. One thousand dollars was expended in the West Philadelphia Crime Prevention Association for on-the-job training. As a result eighty-two persons were placed in jobs in less than a year; sixty more received training and forty-six others attended classes at various levels of education.

The Welfare Rights Organization of Philadelphia received fifteen thousand dollars to help in the organization and mobilization of the poor to fight for their own economic and social rights. Thirty organizers were trained and thirty-five others went into neighborhoods to tell the story of these action groups. So one congregation spread its influence and Christian commitment into its community in a thrilling and dedicated manner. Many other instances can be cited to show how change is possible and how creative the process can be.[5]

There are some specific functions which almost every pastor, minister, or priest is called upon to perform. In almost every instance he is looked upon as the leader of the worshiping community. In public services the church comes together under his direction to offer praise to God, to proclaim its faith in God as

---

[4] See Richard L. Keach, The Purple Pulpit (Valley Forge: Judson Press, 1971) for a more detailed account of the life of this church.

[5] For example, Wallace E. Fisher, From Tradition to Mission (Nashville: Abingdon Press, 1965). Joan Thatcher, The Church Responds (Valley Forge: Judson Press, 1970), describes a number of innovative local churches.

revealed in Christ, to hear the Word proclaimed in Scripture, hymn, anthem, and sermon. He dispenses the sacraments according to the polity and practice of his communion. He celebrates the Mass, presides at the Eucharist, the Communion or the Lord's Supper (all these names are applicable), hears the confessions of his people (again where applicable), baptizes the children (in infant baptism communions) or the candidates (where believer's baptism applies), and dedicates the children or parents.

Paramount to all the worship experiences of the church is the celebration of the Lord's Supper. As Seward Hiltner makes so clear in *Ferment in the Ministry,* there are three facts which have been central to the Protestant concept of celebration. The table has been set with the elements upon it: the minister has been involved in the event ". . . ministering in his name." [6] And there has always been the very clear fact that the laymen are present with the celebrant to share the celebration. These elders, deacons, altar boys, and others play as vital, albeit a different role, as that of the person presiding. "The Communion service emphasizes fellowship and relatedness. It also means 'sharing in.' But fellowship is either reconciling or it is not fellowship at all. . . . In the Communion service, the Kingdom begins now." [7]

A vital part of corporate worship continues to be that of proclamation. The sermon is still an effective means of proclamation but the sermon is changing. The function of the minister as preacher is to expound the Word of God as he opens the Bible in the midst of the congregation. He seeks to relate the eternal truths of Scripture to the contemporary situation so that the Word may be heard as clearly in the 1970's as in the days of Amos or Paul and so that there may be an appropriate response to the Word.

Good preaching has never been a monologue. The part played by an attentive congregation has not always been recognized, but the best preaching of all time has always commanded a response and involved the hearer in the drama of disclosure.

[6] Seward Hiltner, *Ferment in the Ministry* (Nashville: Abingdon Press, 1969), p. 131.

[7] *Ibid.,* p. 133.

The open Bible on the pulpit symbolizes the centrality of the proclamation at the heart of worship.

In many congregations new forms of preaching are being developed. Dialogue sermons are being tried, the question and answer type sermon is used, the open forum is encouraged wherein the congregation meets in an informal session after the formal close of worship to react to the sermon. In some cases groups of lay people are encouraged to sit with the preacher in advance to plan the content and the form of the sermon and to take joint responsibility for its basic thrust. The ministry of preaching may center in one or two members of the staff of the local church, but they do not necessarily carry the total responsibility for this ministry.

The ministry of the local church calls for the minister to participate in the lives of his people at times of joy and triumph; their most lofty aspirations will be shared with him. He will be called upon to confront and sustain them in the Christian fellowship in trials, troubles, bereavements, disasters, and frustrations. As a pastoral visitor in homes, hospitals, and institutions, he will share these crisis occasions of his people. Scarcely a family of his membership will be without some need of his ministry if he is empathetic in his dealings with them, open to discover the real situations of their lives.

The role of the minister as administrator is a controversial one. Many ministers complain that they are theologically trained yet are required to spend a disproportionate amount of their time in administering an institution. It is a certainty that some so-called administration is required of every minister in the local church. Many of them do learn to handle their work in this area; so such administrative work becomes an opportunity and not a burden. Committee work brings one in close touch with fellow members of committees in a peer relationship that can be wholesome, stimulating, and highly rewarding. To share the deeper reasons for the existence and support of the church with a committee can be one of the most challenging situations any minister can develop. Committees do not have to deal only with agendas, with brick and mortar, and with data. They can be helped to see the more ultimate reasons for their "bread and butter" tasks and move progressively into areas that provide satisfaction and challenges not previously uncovered.

The ministry of the pastor touches the lives of people at many points. He will require patience, insight, understanding, and an appreciation of his people. He does not work alone. He is God's man or woman and as such is *called to serve.* He will be enabled to proclaim the Word of God in sermons, in teaching, in the ordinances or sacraments, and in his pastoral relationships. He will, in the old terminology, be the undershepherd of the flock. But as the concepts of the ministry change and develop, the sensitive minister will find many ways of involving his congregation in new and exciting forms of ministry. He will come to look upon his role as that of an enabler, a resource person with specific gifts, skills, and training which will help to mobilize the lay persons of his congregation to perform their rightful ministry. In older thought patterns the minister was the "doer," the primary practitioner. He preached, he taught, he viisted, he advised, he wrote. Now the sensitive, alert clergyman is discovering ways of training others to share this ministry. He sees them as an extension of his outreach, particularly as they make their way out into the world to live out their understanding of the gospel. So in a sense his is the supply function, the mobilizing aspect. He is no longer dependent upon the limits of one pair of hands or of a few hours a day. The laity are involved at a very deep level of commitment that takes seriously the close relationship of devotion, discipleship, and discipline. Success according to these standards is to be measured, not in terms of numbers, but in the degree to which people respond and become committed in depth.

CONFLICTING DEMANDS ON THE MINISTER

Whenever the question of the minister's role in the church and society is raised, one can expect to hear stories of the devastation of conflicting demands. The minister is carefully prepared by his seminary to go into a local congregation or parish and take his place as the spiritual leader of that local manifestation of the church. Soon after he arrives, however, he finds himself performing a variety of tasks or at best administering a program. As he tries to listen to the demands about him, he becomes a consultant to the building or renovation committee; he is responsible for promotion and publicity; he is expected to have at least a rudimentary knowledge of financing and, of course, fund raising; and he may even be expected to sit as the director of a hospital or a residence for senior citizens.

Now before we throw up our hands in horror and despair of ever creating the conditions wherein a person can really find it possible to minister, let us reflect upon several necessary ingredients that must go into the creation of a favorable climate. A survey of the comprehensive ministry in Protestant churches of the U.S.A. led Professor Sam Blizzard to conclude:

> The roles a minister performs in present-day American society are basically equivocal. On the one hand, the Church has a traditional set of norms by which he is expected to be guided. On the other hand, the parishioner has a set of functional expectations by which the minister's professional service is judged. This is the minister's dilemma. . . .
>
> No matter how different ministers' ideas of what is important in the ministry, all wind up doing substantially the same thing. It is perfectly apparent how largely the social roles of Protestant parish ministers are conditioned and defined by the requests of parishioners, the denominational program, and the culture of the community.[8]

Perhaps the stark alternatives set forth in these two paragraphs will provide us with our points of reference.

The Minister's Self-Understanding

As we ask what it is that makes the ministry a Christian vocation; as we seek to clarify what it is that is irreducible in any definition of Christian ministry; and as we ask what it is that makes ministry, ministry, regardless of its form — then we reflect on the words of 1 Peter 2:9:

> You are a chosen race, a royal priesthood, a holy nation, God's own people, that you may declare the wonderful deeds of him who called you out of darkness into his marvelous light.

As we noted in chapter 1, for most persons to be in the ministry is to have responded to the activity of God in their lives. For them their ministry is not so much a vocation as a response, it is

[8] Samuel W. Blizzard, "The Minister's Dilemma" in *The Church and Its Changing Ministry*, ed. Robert C. Johnson (Philadelphia: United Presbyterian Church, 1961), p. 78. Copyright 1956 Christian Century Foundation. Reprinted by permission from the April 25, 1956, issue of *The Christian Century*.

not so much a profession as a way of obedience. The "chosen race" was not composed of a group of persons whose integrity of purpose and singleness of heart was so outstanding that God could do no other than take them for his own. The choice of these people was God's and the power which created and re-created them was also his.

As the people of God experience the meaning of this new life with God, they begin to discover more of the intent of "these wonderful deeds." The "Good News of the Gospel" is translated into the experiences of life and all its demands. The people become imbued with a desire to share their experiences with others. As D. T. Niles has put it, "It is one beggar telling another where to find the bread." From the very beginning, as far back as the church of Antioch, it became very evident that the local congregation of people was a peculiar grouping. They were called Christians and we read in Acts 11 that the people of Antioch began to notice how the Christians loved one another and cared for each other.

The next aspect of the corporate life in the church is that the people of God, in response to the gospel, began to develop a life of service. They committed themselves to the sharing of the Good News in proclamation by word of mouth and in deeds of service. The very essence of the gospel is reflected in the care of the people of God for the needy, the outcast, the widow, the enslaved, and the deposed. Probably the most eloquent sermons preached by most of these followers of the Nazarene were by nature very practical.

If the minister or priest enters into the life of a congregation in such a way as to help it become the chosen people of God, he is able to do so because he is dedicated to a basic understanding of what his ministry must be. He must be aware at all times that the total church is called to minister and not he alone. As he seeks to find his proper place in the ongoing life of his people, he will extend his ministry to such as may become responsive. It is even conceivable that he may so mobilize his congregation that he will find himself out of the "job" to which he was called. And this could be a very good thing.

The minister becomes aware that his main temptation will be

to shape his ministry to the expectations of his people rather than by theological, biblical, or historical truths. He will be driven back to facing the common judgment levied against all ministers that they are preservers of the status quo, mere reflectors of the world around them. How easy it is to judge the worth of a church or the strength of a ministry by the amount of money raised or the number of persons who throng the sanctuary at the appointed hour of Sunday services!

Dr. Elton Trueblood in *The Company of the Committed* aptly illustrates how insidious such a standard of success can be:

> The paradox of the apparent victory, yet real defeat, of the contemporary Church is nowhere more vividly demonstrated than in the present concentration upon *attendance*. Great billboard advertisements appear by the hundreds with a single message, "Worship Together This Week." The fact that the donors of the advertisements are undoubtedly motivated by goodwill toward the life of religion, as they understand it, does not obscure the fundamental ineptitude of their effort. Obviously, the sponsors of the advertisements look upon attendance at a religious assembly as the major religious act or the major evidence of church membership. It is no wonder that they think this, if they observe the frantic and sometimes ingenious efforts of pastors, week by week, to surpass all previous records of attendance.[9]

The Church in the Way

James E. Dittes has written a book by the above title to consider how the church as it is presently constituted is frequently a block rather than a channel of God's blessing.[10] Essentially what Dittes is saying is borne out by the experience of the two-hundred-year-old church located in the inner city of a burgeoning metropolis which is featured in *From Tradition to Mission*.[11] The Lutheran Church of the Holy Trinity, in Lancaster, Pennsylvania, had drifted into a state of nostalgic quiescence, content to remember her glorious days of yore, unwilling to engage actively in the warfare of the present. Wallace Fisher tells how the sleeping giant was awakened and mobilized to be-

[9] Elton Trueblood, *The Company of the Committed* (New York: Harper & Row, Publishers, 1961), pp. 18-19.

[10] James E. Dittes, *The Church in the Way* (New York: Charles Scribner's Sons, 1967).

[11] Wallace E. Fisher, *From Tradition to Mission* (Nashville: Abingdon Press, 1965).

come a center of renewal, involvement, service, and evangelism as the congregation again became aware of the claims of God upon it. In the words of Fisher:

The unconverted parish — a complex of human piety, biblicism, theological naivete, uncritical devotion to an institution and parish activities — confronted by the Word in multiple personal encounters, can be transformed by the Holy Spirit into a dynamic community of persons who employ theology as a tool in fashioning the church's effective ministry.[12]

Some ministers have taken the attitude that the institutional church is an anachronism, that it cannot possibly be redeemed or restored. The old pitchers have to be thrown against the wall. New containers have to be fashioned. As Dr. Trueblood has stated in the opening of Fisher's book, it is refreshing to see "how new life in the existing church is possible, that is great good news." [13] Doubtless there will be many new forms of the church that will emerge and we need not be driven to despair by the inept, shallow, and ineffectual part the church has often chosen to play in today's world. The church stands in the midst of the world to minister to it, to share its hopes and fears, its lot, and to proclaim the transformation possible through the gospel. The Good News must be heard and experienced in the center of today's busy marketplaces. Now let us move to a consideration of some other forms of ministry which usually function on the level of the local congregation.

MULTIPLE STAFF MINISTRIES

In churches where there is a multiple or staff ministry consisting of two or more persons, it is customary to expect some specialization of interests and abilities.

Director of Christian Education

Frequently the first addition made to a one-man ministry is in the area of Christian education. The person chosen may or may not be an ordained man or woman, but the duties are usually designated as being centered in the teaching ministry of the church. The minister or director of Christian education has as his prime responsibility the supervision, coordination, and the continuing support of the life of the congregation as it seeks to

[12] *Ibid.*, pp. 182-183.   [13] *Ibid.*, p. 8, Introduction.

become more involved in the teaching ministry of the Christian church.

Probably the key role of the director of Christian education will be that of leadership development. Adequate leaders need to be discovered, recruited, trained, and then supervised in their work. Many methods of training are possible, such as preservice training in a class situation, periodic training workshops or conferences, and in-service and internship training. In addition to these the director will develop library facilities as a resource to help the willing teacher or leader become more effective in his work.

In chapter 2 the description of the role of the director of Christian education included the necessity for the director to give careful attention to the total curriculum of the church's teaching program in order to keep it abreast of current needs and developments and to ensure that the best resources available are placed in the hands of the staff of the church. The teaching ministry of the local congregation is not aimed solely at children; all members need to be engaged in the teaching-learning process. Nor should it be forgotten that the work of the director, like that of every other person engaged in ministry, is a part of the total life of the church. This involvement in the total church is a misunderstood aspect of the work of Christian education, one which alert ministers can do much to correct.

Pastoral Care

Another form of specialized ministry that is quite frequently found in multiple staff churches is the minister of pastoral care. The person who seeks this role is someone who has found himself to be most effective in the so-called "non-public" functions of the church's ministry. He will spend most of his time encountering the congregation and the community in one-to-one or at most small group situations. It is probable that this man will have special post-seminary training in Clinical Pastoral Education and perhaps in counseling as well.

In close liaison with other members of the team of ministers, the minister of pastoral care will visit parishioners in homes, hospitals, institutions, and within the church building itself. He will, of course, be referred to many of these people because their needs are known to someone in the congregation. Many of these people will be encountered by the minister himself as he does general visitation and discovers crisis situations where his ministry is needed and will be appreciated. When such a ministry becomes established, many persons will seek out such a minister and look to him for guidance and help.

It is not necessary to draw the conclusion that the minister of pastoral care is never to exercise a public ministry. He may very well be an effective preacher or leader of worship; he may have chosen his specialty out of positive attraction to it and not because he was considered deficient in some other area. The close cooperation and liaison with the total staff, which is the hallmark of any effective ministerial team, is especially vital to the ministry of pastoral care. Careful and thorough records and cross-referrals need to be made to ensure that the total congregation is properly served by all members of the staff. When teams of lay people are recruited to conduct pastoral visitation, it is vitally important that the minister in charge be ready to coordinate and consolidate all the visits. He will find very quickly that the lay visitors turn to him to make referrals of one kind or another, and they will expect their calls to be followed up and consummated according to the needs that emerge.

Counseling

Another special ministry that is taking its place among staff ministries is that of counseling. This ministry is frequently performed in the larger churches in urban growth areas and also in Institutes or Centers of Pastoral Counseling which have been and are being established in most of the larger cities. The counselor is a minister, a part of the team; he is usually ordained although this is not a necessity, and he functions within the church or agency which sponsors him and to which he is related.

Most of the people who seek out the pastoral counselor are referred to him by other members of the church staff, by lay people who know of his work and his availability, and by other members of the helping professions in the community, such as doctors, social workers, public health nurses, and hospital personnel. The counselor will be equipped to deal with people on the basis of a more intensive relationship due to his training and the time which he has available. The minister who carries the total responsibility for a parish cannot take the larger amounts of time that counseling frequently requires and still meet his other responsibilities. Of course, there will be times when the pastoral counselor will also make referrals of persons to other community resources, if he feels this is indicated in his assessment of the case.

As noted in regard to other members of a staff ministry, it is absolutely vital for an effective working relationship for all members of the staff to be fully aware of the case load of the counseling minister. The channels of communication need to be kept open at all times so there will be no chance of people working at cross purposes.

Minister of Music

The aspect of ministry that relates most closely to music is carried by persons with a variety of titles. In some cases the title is "Minister of Music," in which case the responsibility is usually a full-time ministry devoted to the integration of music into the total life of a parish or congregation. Much of the work carried on by such a person is related to the choirs of the church and their responsibility to the stated services of worship throughout the church year. The recruiting, training, and support of these choirs is a prime duty. In addition there will need to be close liaison with other team members to assure that the fullest cooperation is achieved for this aspect of the ministry and all other segments.

Parallel experiences in the musical life of a congregation are also a vital part of this ministry. The performance of sacred music in the traditional as well as contemporary media is encouraged, and, in many cases, folk masses, liturgical celebrations, and other forms of religious expression center in the area of music. The youth of every congregation are particularly susceptible to the wiles of music, and the ministry of music is frequently found in close cooperation with and support of the ministry with youth. The contributions of musical people can be made in an exceptional degree in camping and other summer experiences, so the ministry of music need not be confined to the local church.

TEAM MINISTRIES

The term "team ministry" has been used, but we need to be clear about its meaning. Some communions have long and honorable histories of multiple staff ministries but these are not always "team" ministries. This is not just a semantic quibble. Frequently one senior minister is charged with the responsibility of "running a parish program." He has assistants or associates for whom he is responsible and to whom he assigns tasks and areas of responsibility. Some of these situations are in fact teams; many of them are something quite other.

A team ministry that is fully operative takes into account the full potential of every staff member and the positive contribution he or she can make to the total life of the congregation. Formal administrative structures are relegated to the periphery (as much as this is humanly possible), and every person is looked upon as equally valuable to the corporate life of the ministry.

For example, Eastwood Baptist Mission in the North End of Hamilton, Ontario, has employed a young woman as a "girl Friday." She is a receptionist and a referral source. She keeps records and files and manages a great deal that transpires in the total life of the mission. Her contribution is invaluable and she sits in on all evaluation and planning sessions to make her own contribution to the team ministry.

Frequent planning and evaluation sessions are required to foster mutual understanding of the total thrust of mission. Plans in each responsibility area are merged into the totality of planning and each is evaluated in the light of current developments. There is no place for the prima donna, the insecure, or the dictator. Indeed, one needs to be very much aware of his own personality dynamics before one moves into such a team ministry. The potential is unlimited and the rewards are great. The role expectancy of both minister and congregation, however, has a tendency to stand in the way of total effectiveness.

Herman J. Sweet in his book *The Multiple Staff in the Local Church* deals with many of the issues surrounding multiple staffs.

Perhaps his analysis of this one aspect is most helpful at this point.

> It should be possible to develop staff relationships that open the way for all members of the congregation to relate to the whole staff. The united ministry should be made manifest through each member of the staff. Members of the flock should find in each staff member a channel to any other staff member whose particular leadership or ministry meets their needs, and they should be able to sense that the care of souls, which they may have assumed to be the chief responsibility of the senior pastor, is in fact the central concern in the ministry of the whole staff. Thus, in a sense at least, pastoral care is extended and multiplied and comes to have many facets without being departmentalized.[14]

It is probably not necessary here to expand on the development, but it ought to be noted that not all team ministries are located in one parish or church situation. There are several excellent examples of "larger-parish" plans or cooperative units where three to five or more people staff six, seven, or eight churches with relatively small congregations and where their cooperative ministry allows each of them to contribute his or her particular talent to the total ministerial team. This approach can be of great value in rural areas or in the inner-city parishes where the number of adherents is small and the needs diverse. Close liaison between the participating units is vital if the service aspects of ministry are to be greatly expanded and much fuller resources are to be made available to the member units.

As one contemplates the variety of gifts that may be exercised in a team setting, one needs always to bear in mind the operative fact of God working through human instrumentality and enabling each instrument to become a part of the great symphony of praise to God's glory. The testimony of Paul sums it all up: "I worked harder than any of them, though it was not I, but the grace of God which is with me" (1 Corinthians 15:10).

Each church exists to proclaim the reconciling purpose of God in Christ, and each act of ministry must be motivated by a desire to further this cause and out of an obedient awareness that it is in faithful discipleship that the Body of Christ lives. So God is served in the midst of his world.

[14] Herman J. Sweet, *The Multiple Staff in the Local Church* (Philadelphia: The Westminster Press, 1963), pp. 20-21. Copyright © MCMLXIII, W. L. Jenkins. Used by permission.

4 Ministries Beyond the Walls

> "I am persuaded that neither death, nor life . . .
> shall be able to separate us from the love of God,
> which is in Christ Jesus our Lord."
> Romans 8:31

We are perfectly aware of the encouraging fact that many local congregations are ill at ease confined within the "four walls" of their building. Encouraging stories are heard almost daily of the imaginative and thrilling ways in which walls are being breached and the gospel message, as embodied in the living representatives, taken abroad. The Potter's House, a coffee house sponsored by the Church of the Saviour, Washington, D.C., is a good example of how an obedient congregation has moved out into an area of need and sought to relate its faith to that need.[1]

In this chapter we will look at some of the more established of the dispersed ministries that are available, most of which operate from a base other than the local church or parish. A great many of these opportunities for ministry are under the sponsorship of councils or associations of churches. Some dioceses, presbyteries, and associations are making appointments; and in more and more instances councils of churches are moving to make such appointments. Obviously we will not be able to deal with all of these forms of ministry, but we will concentrate on the more representative ones.

THE CHAPLAINCY

The role of the chaplain is a relatively new one as compared with some other forms of ministry. It is now, however, a firmly

[1] See Elizabeth O'Connor, *Call to Commitment* (New York: Harper & Row, Publishers, 1963).

established and widely accepted avenue of service. Chaplains function in many settings: jails, hospitals, institutions, and on most university campuses. One hospital chaplain stated his assessment of his vocation in this way: "I often feel that this work is more nearly in the mainstream of the Church's mission in the world than much of the parish church life I see reflected in our patients." [2]

The Hospital Chaplain

From the time that Anton T. Boisen began to pioneer in the field of chaplaincy at the Massachusetts State Hospital in Worcester, Massachusetts, there has been a marked development of and acceptance of the place of the chaplain in the treatment team of the hospital. The description of the chaplaincy in chapter 2 outlines the educational requirements laid down by the accrediting agencies for a recognized chaplain. He must go beyond the ordination requirements of his denomination and equip himself with clinical training which is done in residency in an approved hospital or institution and which includes in the latter stages participation in the teaching of the skills of the pastoral office. Dr. Ernest E. Bruder points out in his excellent little book that some hospitals require their staff members to go beyond this level and to undergo psychiatric evaluation of their own personalities.[3] He quotes with approval the catalog of The Washington School:

"The Fellows of The School hold that no person may be entrusted with responsibility for therapeutic intervention in difficulties in living who shall not have undergone a searching scrutiny of his personal history, liabilities and assets from the therapeutic standpoint. In view of this basic premise in all training programs in The School, emphasis is laid on individual psychiatric counseling, taking into consideration the needs of the respective candidates in relation to the fields in which they seek training." [4]

The hospital chaplain is called upon to minister to persons involved in the crisis of illness or accident. He takes his place in the hospital setting and is available to people on request or re-

---

[2] Robert B. Reeves, Jr., "The Chaplaincy and the Church's Mission," *Pastoral Psychology*, June, 1966, p. 6.

[3] Ernest E. Bruder, *Ministering to Deeply Troubled People* (Englewood Cliffs, N.J.: Prentice-Hall, Inc., 1963).

[4] *Ibid.*, p. 19.

ferral the same as many other staff persons. Sometimes the chaplain will see an ambulance drive up to the emergency entrance and will witness the entry of a patient on a stretcher. As the door of the emergency ward closes, he will discover that the next of kin of the patient have also arrived and are in the waiting room. They are distraught, completely unnerved by their crisis, and are more than ready to encounter the chaplain who is ready to minister to them and their loved one. The chaplain sees his parish as consisting of all persons within the hospital complex who look to him for ministry. This includes patients, family, and friends, those related through clinics and extension programs, and the staff. For the most part the relationship of the chaplain is one-to-one with the patient.

The chaplain does not see every person who comes into the hospital in a routine manner. His services are requested by patients through the staff, most frequently nurses, or directly by phone. Sometimes members of the family or friends will speak to him and request his services. On certain specialty services the chaplain may accompany the doctors and others on their rounds. Here he contributes his knowledge of the patient to that of other team members and helps in the assessment and diagnosis. In some other services it may be customary for the chaplain to meet in "milieu therapy" sessions as a member of a treatment team. Here he can contribute more directly as he functions in consultation with other specialists.

Most hospitals have the means of informing the staff of those who are critically ill. The chaplain's office receives daily communication to this effect and direct follow-up becomes possible. It is frequently in these situations that the ministry of the chaplain to the ill person and his family is most requested. The issues of life and death are ever present in the hospital setting and sometimes the chaplain has opportunity to bring people to a realistic assessment of the meaning of death.

One of the most basic aspects of the life of the chaplain comes out of his relationship to the staff of the hospital. The chaplain is seen as a confidant and counselor, and his support is sought in the midst of problems, perplexities, and frustrations. Many hospitals invite the chaplain to meet with nurses in their training or orientation sessions to help them to see his perspectives and to broaden their own. Issues of ethical implications, life, death, bereavement, separation, loneliness — all of these and more are raised in the context of the hospital's life. The chaplain who can help the nursing staff to be sensitive to their patients in these areas has gone a long way toward the establishment of the climate he seeks to create as he works with the hospital administration.

Sometimes this function becomes more formalized in hospitals where the chaplain is an accredited Supervisor of Clinical Training. He will have a group of ministers, some seminarians and others from pastorates, under his direction who are seeking to broaden their understanding of ministry. He will arrange to conduct lectures and seminars with leading members of the hospital's team, and he will supervise the work of the trainees as they are assigned to various parts of the hospital as "Chaplains-in-Training."

Occasionally the chaplain will cooperate with another staff person, such as a psychiatrist, to carry on a special seminarian series. The University of Chicago Hospitals and Clinics had such a seminar called "On Death and Dying." [5] There Dr. Elisabeth Kübler-Ross carried on research designed to clarify many of the issues concerned with patients who have been told that their illnesses are terminal. In cooperation with one of the chaplains, the Rev. Carl Nighswonger, Dr. Ross conducts interviews with patients in a special room (one-way glass is installed) that can be viewed by the seminar group, and immediately afterward the interview is evaluated at some length. The results of such a teaching seminar are most clearly felt in the staff levels of the hospitals. Many of the unnamed, unrecognized fears surrounding serious illness and death are discussed, and more positive attitudes are developed which are more healthy and more conducive to openness and treatment.

Various opportunities for worship are offered to the hospital community throughout the year, with special importance given to the festival occasions of the church year. These services are

[5] See Elisabeth Kubler-Ross, *On Death and Dying* (New York: Crowell, Collier MacMillan, Inc., 1969) for details.

usually brief and to the point; the sermons are short and pithy. In almost all hospitals the chaplain stands ready to administer the sacraments or to have a priest or pastor from the community available on request. Such matters as confession and the administering of the last rites are arranged on a similar basis. Chapels as places of worship and quiet meditation are available, and supplies of devotional literature are placed in readily accessible racks for those who wish them. As he prepares a service of worship, the chaplain is aware that staff members as well as patients and their families will be in attendance.

The life of the hospital chaplain may best be summed up in a conversation recorded by Joseph E. McCabe:

"Yes, in any one day here you encounter the happiness of new life and the emptiness of life where an older person is eager to be away. I congratulate new parents here, and in my prayer with them I express thanksgiving to God for this new life. Then I may go directly to surgical and sit with a family circle that has been broken by death. In each case it is not I as a person they need, but spiritual reality, and God mediates that spiritual reality through the chaplain, if his own life is really open and free and securely anchored to Christ." [6]

Further specialization is possible for chaplains who take up the particular problems related to mental illness, retardation, rehabilitation, and others. People interested in these areas can find source material which will detail the requirements and potential. As an example, a careful reading of *Ministering to Deeply Troubled People*[7] will provide an overview of the problems related to the treatment of mental illness and the peculiar contribution the minister or chaplain can make to that treatment. A special issue of *Pastoral Psychology* edited by Virginia Kreyer[8] dealt with the special problems of those who are physically handicapped.

Chaplains in Prisons and Reform Institutions

The church has tried to bear in mind the needs of those who

---

[6] Joseph E. McCabe, *Challenging Careers in the Church* (New York: McGraw-Hill Book Company, 1966), pp. 86-87. Used with permission of McGraw-Hill Book Company.

[7] Bruder, *op. cit.*

[8] *Pastoral Psychology,* June, 1965.

have been convicted of some crime and have been imprisoned by society in the hope of their restoration to that society in a reformed condition. In this area the sensitive contribution of the chaplain can be the means for the communication of forgiveness and renewal.

As in the work of the hospital chaplain, the reform institution setting lends itself most readily to a one-to-one relationship. As many of the prisoners are incarcerated for long periods of time, the chaplain has time to develop relationships in greater depth than is possible in other settings. He will be called upon to minister to the basic human needs that arise out of imprisonment. The alienation and loneliness of separation from community and family; the unnatural environment and the problems attendant upon an all-male or all-female society; the strange and ominous prison-life society with its echelons of power and authority — all of these and more will be presented to the chaplain for his ministrations.

Again, the interest of the perceptive chaplain will not be confined to that of the prisoners, but he will be called upon to minister to the total staff in ways which emerge peculiarly from such an environment. He will be able to work with those who need to make assessments of prisoners and those charged with the responsibility for recommending and supervising paroles. He will be able to provide valuable assistance to those workers interested in rehabilitation, helping them aid prisoners build bridges back to the world. The total milieu of every prison leaves a great deal to be desired. Without becoming aligned with any faction the chaplain can work for better treatment conditions and greatly enhance true communication from all sides.

The prison chaplain will frequently find himself called upon to be an interpreter and go-between for the prisoner and his family. In a high percentage of cases he will find that he is dealing with prisoners who are basically alienated from their society and from their family in particular. If the prisoner's return is to hold hope for rehabilitation, a great many attitudes besides those of the prisoner will need to change; and it is here that the chaplain finds a fruitful area for ministry.

Opportunities for group study and worship present them-selves in the penal system. Occasionally the chaplain arranges for key people from the community to come into the prison and to serve as resource persons for study and worship. Compulsory worship always presents some problems but even here it can be handled with integrity and purpose by the sensitive chaplain.

> "Men come to services for the best and the worst reasons. Some are sincerely religious, others come just to break the monotony. As a chaplain you take what you get and hope something good is happening for some of them. Last Sunday I spoke about Peter's denial of his Lord, and how when they met next time Christ did not accuse him or reject him, but took him back, and trusted him and used him mightily. Then on Tuesday when I visited the kitchen, one of the bakers came over to me and said he had determined that Peter's story would come true again in his own life. It's worth a year's work to hear a college graduate who is doing time for forgery make a statement like that." [9]

Other chaplaincies are available in different types of prisons, detention homes, or penitentiaries. Some of these are part-time and are carried on by local pastors or priests in connection with the work of a parish. Each situation should be investigated on its own merits by those interested in such a ministry.

Military Chaplains

Unfortunately the necessity still exists for large numbers of men and women to be engaged in the defense of their countries in the armed forces. These are a mobile group of people whom the church has sought to serve through the chaplaincy. Most of those who hold appointments as military chaplains do so on the recommendation of their own denomination or communion. Protestant chaplains serve without reference to their denominations and are simply designated as "Protestant" chaplains. The Roman Catholic and Jewish chaplains carry the designation of their faith.

The problems of a highly mobile and multi-faceted constituency are all present to the military chaplain. Except for a very few headquarters bases, his constituency is a rapidly changing one and his contacts tend to be more superficial than those of the parish or institutionally based ministry. All of the problems

[9] McCabe, *op. cit.*, p. 90.

of displacement are his as people are removed peremptorily from their familiar surroundings and life and are transplanted to new surroundings.

All of the usual functions of a parish minister are performed by the military chaplain. He commonly ministers to the base personnel and, in many cases, to the families of servicemen who are housed in a nearby settlement except, of course, on some overseas assignments or in theaters of war. The chaplain christens or baptizes; he administers the sacraments, presides at services of marriage, buries, and provides opportunities for study and worship.

Because of the physical separation of armed forces personnel from their families, a larger percentage of compassionate issues need to be dealt with by the military chaplain. He will be concerned about changes in families caused by death or sudden illness which radically alter the families' ability to cope with life. For example, the sudden invaliding of a farmer father may leave the family totally without support and the services of the chaplain may be sought to intervene on behalf of the serviceman affected. A discharge on compassionate grounds may become necessary. Illnesses or other catastrophes may strike the serviceman's dependents at any time. The chaplain will be requested to secure leave privilege through the approved channels in order to allow the men to make whatever arrangements are necessary.

Preparation for the return to civilian life is an area of emphasis in which the alert chaplain can make a valuable contribution. There are real problems for many armed forces personnel in moving back to civilian life. Consider the question of occupation and location. What are the possibilities open to someone who has been absent for two, three, or fifteen years for moving into a certain job? Does he require further training to qualify and if so how does he go about determining the wisdom of such a move? There are career counselors available, but the chaplain is frequently the one approached and he can offer valuable help. Armed forces personnel retire at a relatively low age and this fact raises a whole battery of problems rather unique to the military. Parenthetically, some people of decided Christian commitment look upon their retirement as the opportunity for full-time service in a church or church-related agency. As his military pension frees such a person from some of the worries of remuneration, he is able to serve in places that cannot otherwise support a full-time ministry. The chaplain can be of inestimable strength in counseling such persons.

In a theater of war the work of the chaplain takes on a demand basis. He moves with the troops and is interested to minister to them from the background of his faith and Christian commitment as related to the horrors, trauma, and catastrophe of conflict. The hurt and fractured are a prime concern and the base hospital is a frequent site of ministry. The shocked, fatigued, and deranged frequently need immediate ministry and repatriation. The chaplain has occasion on many fronts to join other personnel in ministering to civilian persons who have been disrupted and shattered by war. Children and older persons are some of the earliest casualties and a ministry to such persons is clearly indicated. On a combat assignment the chaplain travels light and of necessity carries most of the visible symbols of his office with him. He personifies the presence of Christ and that of his church and in so doing performs a crisis ministry of tremendous importance.

Campus Chaplains

In recent years the church has looked to its responsibility to the university and college communities and has sought to redefine its ministry there. On the campus are to be found all of the confusion, frustration, and excitement of the "multi-versity." On campus there are virtually unlimited possibilities for growth, discovery, and stimulation; but as is all too evident, there is also disruption, disillusionment, frustration, despair, a sense of insignificance, and impotence. The problems of bureaucracy and the attendant impersonality of the larger campus and the felt inaccessibility of many faculty members, all provide the backdrop against which the college chaplain operates.

One chaplaincy group in its annual report summed up the ethos of the university by saying:

Clearly the need to explore the personal dimensions of learning becomes of primary importance in such a situation. Equally important, too, are questions about the overall purpose and direction of issues of education and research. Where these concerns are not taken up by the university, one witnesses a rejection of the institution and its goals — a rejection which may manifest itself in a revolutionary anti-institutionalism, or in an indifference toward education, resulting in a passive and safe acquiescence to the demands of the institution. Many very creative young people are therefore faced with "dropping out" as an authentic option for them.[10]

As with the hospital and military chaplains, the campus ministry is frequently carried on without reference to denominational labels. Representatives of most of the major denominations and communions are usually present to respond to requests for services that relate specifically to one communion. The celebration of the Mass, confession, the Eucharist, baptisms, and marriage, are all an integral part of campus ministry. Most of the less specific one-to-one encounters and the group experiences are shared by all the chaplains on campus. The scope of the chaplains' work embraces everything from personal counseling with the very prevalent and burning issues of self-identity through issues related to a stand of "conscientious objection" or pacifism, to say nothing of the moral issues raised in our multi-faceted and pluralistic society.

University years are a time of transition and adjustment for young people. Some parents still look upon the university authorities as surrogate parents and they express tremendous anxiety when they discover that this expectation is not being fulfilled. For some students university provides a chance to make a radical break with the established patterns of home, the community, and the church. For some this rebellion is quiet and well reasoned; for others it is quite overt and radical. For many of these young people the chaplain stands both as a link with their past and as a buffer against it. Out of this representative capacity many opportunities for ministry arise. As the student seeks to choose from among the wide range of possibilities that present themselves, he is open to those who will hear him and will listen with purpose and give help to clarify and evaluate. The approach of the chaplain may seem highly tentative and experimental, for it must vary from year to year, in fact from day to day. Always it is pastoral in intent and is frequently centered in a parish

[10] Mimeographed report.

house that is clearly open, friendly, and available to all who desire to make it their resource. Periodic special emphasis weeks based on the arts, the crisis of faith, and film or TV discussion groups provide avenues of entrée to student and faculty contacts.

Most campus chaplains provide opportunities for both corporate and informal worship. It must be admitted that experiences vary greatly. On many campuses the work of the chaplains during the week is probably more effective than what transpires on Sunday, although it is all part of one ministry. Some chaplains hold teaching posts in the university as a regular part of their duties. The relationship of the chaplain to student groups of Christian persuasion is a vital one. Campus chaplains cooperate with one another and keep the lines of communication open as they all seek to serve the total university community. Some churches located on the edge of a campus seek to operate in a dual capacity serving both the community and college. The "town-gown" issues are evident but many churches are coping with the dual role and are ministering with distinction.

COUNSELING CENTERS

Another recent extension to ministry has occurred with the development of pastoral counseling as a specialty. In most urban areas pastoral institutes or centers have been established. Most of these centers have the support and cooperation of the major denominations and communions and are considered as a vital support ministry to which referrals are made and from whom consultative help is available. In some cases, as the Marble Collegiate Church in New York City, the center is integrally related to one church and its pastoral ministry. This relationship does not necessitate the center being totally dependent upon the church for its support nor does it preclude a separate corporate entity. In other cases, as the Pastoral Institute in Calgary, Alberta, the center is developed as an interfaith, interdisciplinary ministry of the churches. The Pastoral Institute includes physicians, social workers, educators, pastors, counselors, clerks, secretaries, volunteers, and staff. A wide range of counseling services is made available through the institute, such as marriage education, marriage counseling, behavior assessment, and temperament analysis. In addition, a great deal of time and energy is expended in the training program of the institute in which gifted persons are encouraged to develop and use their skills in counseling.

In the field of pastoral counseling the genius of this type of ministry is enhanced by the long tradition of pastoral care. Clebsch and Jaekle in their review of pastoral care as it developed across the centuries identify four major distinctives of pastoral care:

a) *Healing* — "a pastoral function that aims to overcome some impairment by restoring the person to wholeness and by leading him to advance beyond his previous condition." [11]

b) *Sustaining* — helping a hurting person to endure and to transcend a circumstance in which restoration to his former condition or recuperation from his malady is either impossible or so remote as to seem improbable.

c) *Guiding* — assisting perplexed persons to make confident choices between alternative courses of thought and action, when such choices are viewed as affecting the present and future state of the soul.

d) *Reconciling* — seeks to re-establish broken relationships between man and fellowman and between man and God. Historically reconciling has employed two modes — forgiveness and discipline.[12]

Every attempt is made, therefore, to keep the centers of pastoral counseling *pastoral* in every sense of that term. The average parish priest or minister, even if he is highly skilled in the competencies of counseling, does not have the time needed to undertake a large counseling load. If he tried to carry individual or conjoint family and group counseling, he would soon be aware of great areas of neglect in his parish work. Thus specialty centers have developed and are meeting a vital need for this specialized ministry.

HALFWAY HOUSES

Under this interesting rubric may be grouped a number of ministries which seek to be available to persons halfway between certain institutions and the community. Probably the first notion of this approach came through sheltered workshops and centers for crippled and/or retarded workers. Now a rather broad spec-

[11] William A. Clebsch and Charles R. Jaekle, *Pastoral Care in Historical Perspective* (Englewood Cliffs, N.J.: Prentice-Hall, Inc., 1964), p. 33.

[12] *Ibid.*, pp. 32-66.

trum of such agencies is developing to cope with problems of alcoholism, drug addiction, and delinquency and to help persons returning to society after serving a prison sentence.

"Easy does it" may be the slogan for such centers. Total and sudden immersion back into society for someone who has sought treatment for the problems of alcoholism is just too big a package to be handled successfully. Sometimes if a person can move out of a treatment center and can be housed in a *Halfway House,* he can move back at a more reasonable pace and still can look to the agency for the supportive therapy that he needs. For the most part it is expected that his active treatment will be completed, but in the Halfway situation he will be associated with helping persons who know what issues he will face and who are ready to help him to cope, to stand on his own feet, and to become totally rehabilitated. The association with others who have moved through the same cycles is a further source of encouragement to him. Residency in these units is not usually of long duration and the length of stay will vary from person to person. Not every one will progress at an even pace and some may experience a relapse. Those who seek to minister in such surroundings will need patience and a realistic assessment of their potential. The success rates are not dramatic and one needs to be thoroughly aware of this aspect when one enters such an area of service. Those who are dealing with drug and alcohol related problems will need to expect relatively low returns on the success scale. The victories will be all the sweeter because they will be hard won and appreciated.

Not quite in the same category but certainly related to the Halfway House are the gang workers and others who seek to meet the "dropout" youth in their mobile and highly explosive society. Some workers in large cities move out onto the streets and attach themselves to whatever grouping allows them to establish a relationship. Others move into the areas where there are clearly defined congregations of floating youth and seek to establish outposts of communication. Many times these workers use a refurbished house which a group of concerned and interested citizens has taken over in a run-down district. The House of Zodiac, in Regina, Saskatchewan, is financed on an ad hoc basis by the Youth Committee of the city. Campus organizations help pay the rent, and lawyers, police, and others lend their support.

The House of Zodiac grew out of a desire on the part of several high school graduates to have a place of their own. Those responsible for its establishment hope to keep the relationships between the police and the youth at a manageable level. The house for transient youth is headed by a young, 240-pound giant, Gary Stewart, who looks upon this as his opportunity to do something tangible and important for these kids. "It is a hostel for transients only," Mr. Stewart explained. "No one can stay longer than three nights. If people can pay, they pay what they can; otherwise they pay nothing."

"These kids don't fit in the Salvation Army thing," said Mr. Gosse, one of the Board of Advisors. He admits they often don't fit in the YMCA thing either. "It's not a Y show; it's their show." [13]

The terms of reference for House of Zodiac are rather loose and ill-defined, of necessity. In that regard it is a pretty clear reflection of a number of such ventures that have sprung up here and there across the country. Another member of the Advisory Board of House of Zodiac summed it up:

> We've got to deal with a fact of life, there are thousands of young people who haven't completed high school. They aren't criminals. They're here and they're on the streets. Let's talk to them, find out what they can do, and what they can do for us.
>
> We're a little oversensitive about many of our sacred cows, and we're short changing ourselves if we can't sit down and talk with the young people. [14]

On a more established level, the work of the Salvation Army is probably the best known. For decades the Army has worked with the dispossessed, the alcoholic, the down-and-out, the addicted, the poor and unfortunate of society. The work of the "Army" is changing, too, but the citadels and outposts which it mans are outstanding examples of ministry "beyond the walls."

SEMINARIES AND COLLEGES

At another level again for a large number of people there is

---

[13] Douglas Sagin, article in *Toronto Globe & Mail*, Friday, June 12, 1970.
[14] *Ibid.*

a viable form of ministry in teaching. At the outset most colleges were under the general aegis of the church. For the most part now colleges have become private institutions and are open for enrollment to all who are interested. Usually many openings exist for qualified personnel in teaching at several levels of education. Because of various circumstances, there are times when the supply of teachers exceeds the demand for them.

At the elementary and secondary school level in institutions sponsored by the church, there are openings in almost every area of academic pursuit. At the college and university levels specialists are in demand who are competent in their field but who also share something of the Christian commitment of the college in which they teach. Opportunities to teach religious knowledge or subjects related to comparative religion exist in some institutions. In the discussion on ministries and missions in the chapter *Experimental Ministries* more will be said about the opportunities for teaching in the overseas work of the church. This area of service is a vital area of interest to potential teachers both for long-term assignment and also for terms of from two to five years.

The field of *seminary teaching* is not a large one and it is well to be realistic if one's aspirations tend in this direction. Most seminaries are staffed by persons who hold earned doctoral degrees and who are competent in a particular field of study, such as Church History, New Testament, Homiletics, Theology, Christian Ethics, or World Church. In addition the majority of these people have had experience in the life of the church at some level, often the local church, and are ordained clergy, fully accredited members of their own denominations. It is probably fair to say that the majority of seminary professors did not set out to achieve this role from the beginning of their training. Most of them became aware of certain talents, aptitudes, and interests as they pursued their education. Indeed, for many of them the job sought *them*, they did not seek out the job. To be aware of the possibilities of seminary teaching is one thing; to aspire to it without looking at some of the alternatives is another. The wise hunter will probably not stake his whole expedition on the successful flight of one arrow or one bullet.

DENOMINATIONAL STAFF

One of the most prominent groups of persons whose labors are performed "Beyond the Walls" are those who are employed by denominational or interdenominational bodies. These people form the "bureaucracies" of each section of the denominational structure. It is impossible to list the variety of ministries performed by such persons. A brief listing of the basic thrust of their labors is given here:

EXECUTIVES — At the national, state or provincial, and city level there are those who are charged with the administration of the business of the church's life. Coordination of effort, communication of ideas, consolidation of resources — all of these are part of the executives' role.

Some staff members are specifically charged to raise the funds necessary for the continuance of programs. Some deal with promotion of programs; some are educational officers and developers of curriculum.

FIELD REPRESENTATIVES — These are the staff members whose responsibility it is to get out among the constituents, to implement decisions and programs, and to provide counsel and support to local churches. It is an equally important role for such persons to listen to the "grass-root" opinions and to keep open the lines of communication with headquarters. Bare directives, even when formulated on the basis of opinions expressed by a constituency, need a great deal of interpretation. It is the field staff members who carry this responsibility.

SPECIAL INTERESTS — In addition to the generalists there must be those who do special things. Some, as already mentioned, will be responsible for the development and implementation of curriculum. They will make available to the users of their materials and resources training opportunities and workshop events. Clusters of workers will be called together to share new ideas and to explore better ways of teaching, leading, or directing. Some will have their special emphasis in evangelism, missions (home and overseas), social action, urban affairs, schools and colleges, or hospitals and institutions. All of these and others provide opportunities for specialized ministries.

5 Experimental Ministries

Indeed, the Church has a future; it has *the* future. This is the eighth day which passes description and cannot be foreseen, the day on which God will complete his work of creation, the Church will reach the goal of its pilgrimage and the world will recognize its Lord. "And that seventh day will be our sabbath, a day that knows no evening, but is followed by the day of the Lord, an everlasting eighth day, hallowed by the resurrection of Christ, prefiguring the eternal rest not only of the spirit, but of the body as well. Then we shall have holiday and we shall see, we shall see and we shall love, we shall love and we shall praise. Behold, this is how it shall be at the end without end. For what else is our end, but to come to that kingdom which has no end?" [1]

Many people who are engaged in what we have called *Ministries Beyond the Walls* would view their work as experimental. But most of them see very little indication that they are establishing any long-range trends for the church's expression of its ministry. However, in fact, many of those people are at the forefront of the push to keep the church at the business of self-evaluation and experimentation.

A second facet of this whole issue has to do more directly with ministry itself. A generation ago it was the rare student who did not look upon his calling as a lifetime vocation to be served in the settled ministry of a local church or in one of the missionary agencies of the denomination. Today such an aspiration is far less common. Rather we are hearing about young people giving

[1] Hans Kung, *The Church*, © Verlag Herder KG Freiburg im Breisgau 1967, English translation © Burns & Oates Ltd., 1967, published by Sheed & Ward Inc., N.Y.

their undivided allegiance to a particular form of ministry for periods of five or ten years, rarely more, and frequently less. Their long-term aims have not been clearly articulated, but they expect to move on to some other vocation once they have "done their thing." Without making qualitative judgments about this trend, or endorsing either alternative, we do need to recognize this discernable trend if we are to see the picture with some wholeness.

The term "experimental ministries" covers a wide spectrum of ministries ranging from those carried on by individual persons or churches to those of rather large proportions in which several communions cooperate and participate. For those who are contemplating a ministry in such an area let it be clearly understood that the life cycle of such experiments is relatively short. To be very specific, one would be rather crestfallen to prepare oneself to work with a coffee house ministry among dock workers or sailors, if in the interim there was a possibility that that particular coffee house would be supplemented by a newer and more viable vehicle.

Also, most experimental ministries are indigenous and grow up out of a special need that develops on location. This is not to say that these ministries are not valid expressions, but is intended to emphasize the fact that they are not easily duplicated elsewhere. The East Harlem Protestant Parish, for example, is unique and particular in its own way. It is highly unlikely that it could be, or even should be, "transplanted" to St. Paul, Minnesota, or Vancouver, B.C. The Potter's House coffee shop of the Church of the Saviour, Washington, D.C., is a remarkable phenomenon in its own right. Again, though, it is unlikely that it could be reproduced *as is* in another part of the continent.

The Church at Westmount near London, Ontario, is an embryonic approach to ministry that gives great promise for the future. Under the guidance of a recent seminary graduate, a small group of people secured a farm property on the edge of the suburban sprawl of London. From the very beginning the emphasis was on the potential of small group encounter. No formal services or programs were envisaged. People came to seek the ways and means of making their faith more relevant in their lives and to covenant with others who shared in this purpose.

On Sundays thirty to forty people sit in what was once the farmhouse living room. Their time together is spent in study, worship, discovery, prayer, and research. They meet as families and only the very youngest are accommodated elsewhere. The minister did not seek ordination in his denomination for two years after graduation because he feared that it would set him apart from the lay people of the church community, and he did not want this to happen. Youth gatherings are held at various times, and during the week study and encounter groups meet; other groupings concern themselves with the arts and hobbies. Wherever the interest is, there Westmount seeks to meet the people. This form of ministry promises much for the future.

The main value of an examination of these experimental ministries to the person looking toward them for guidance is that they can be "paradigms" or perhaps "models." They do give some strong evidence of why they are meeting needs, reaching people, eliciting response, "getting the message across," or however we describe it. These experimenters call for a type of reformation (re-formation, that is) of ministry in the church that will plunge deeply into the contemporary issues and determine how in proclaiming the gospel the church can become indeed "the pilgrim people of God."

THE LARGER CONTEXT

The outcry for renewal was heard at the meetings of the World Council of Churches at Uppsala, July, 1968, as it directed its attention to "Renewal in Mission." Once again it was emphasized that an unbelievable contrast exists between the two billion people of the world who do not follow the Christian religion and those millions who do. What restructuring and rethinking ought to take place on the part of the white Christians who engage black cultures in dialogue? What replies can we make to the "insistent and poignant cries from all continents on behalf of the underprivileged, those who suffer because of a deprivation of food, justice and knowledge?" [2] The church needs to become

[2] Manuscript published privately by McMaster Divinity College.

aware of the great issues involved in the growth and development of nations and in the contrast between the technologically developed nations and those which are still struggling to emerge into the twentieth century. "The Church has a prime responsibility to be the prophetic voice that condemns any attitudes of complacency, self-satisfaction or isolation." [3] The church is always called to be the servant body of Christ, not a spiritual ghetto.

The strategy of overseas missions is changing. For example, the Baptist Overseas Mission Board and the Baptist Convention of Ontario and Quebec have just concurred with the request of the Kenya Christian Council (known as the African Christian Church and Schools) to send missionary personnel to that country to give help at specific points. This request has stated very clearly that the intent of the Council is to keep total control of its own operation and to utilize such experience and skills of Canadian personnel as they request for a period of up to ten years. The primary emphasis at the moment is the establishing of schools and clinics, and the first people to go will be teachers of teachers and other resource persons.

> The African Christian Church and Schools have developed without missionary assistance for more than twenty years but the leaders now feel that they could benefit from the help of a few missionaries — such as an educational missionary to help them establish a Christian secondary school, a missionary who will help them to get their young people organized and trained for Christian service, etc. . . . [4]

The Baptist Convention leaders have the total commitment of their Kenyan brothers that they will provide the physical facilities for the operation and the personnel to be trained. The Baptists of Canada have been asked to recruit the best people to meet these specific needs.

Related to this request from Kenya, the missionary strategy of all communions is in such a state of flux that the Board of Overseas Missions has requested carte blanche approval to deploy its total staff of missionaries any place in the world where there is need and opportunity. Some countries are being closed

---

[3] *Ibid.*, p. 93.
[4] *Canadian Baptist Overseas Mission Report,* June, 1970.

to Christian missionaries while other avenues are opening. It is quite clear that the comity arrangements which formerly settled the allocation of predetermined areas to certain denominational groups as their fields of service are no longer possible.

Some of these attempts to meet special needs will of necessity be experimental and of short duration. Some will be turned over to indigenous leadership as soon as possible. Some will even be phased out as inadequate. We can predict with some assurance that most will be relatively short lived and subject to constant scrutiny and periodic evaluation. Many exciting possibilities will present themselves. Persons interested in short-term assignments will be the ones most likely to be attracted to these opportunities for ministry.

MINISTRIES AND MISSION

Peter Berger has told of the priest who was working in a slum section of a European city and when asked why he was doing it, he replied, "So that the rumor of God may not disappear completely." [5]

Fortunately the words "Home" and "Foreign" missions no longer are used, but we still speak of overseas missions and home missions. The real point that needs clarification, however, is that we are not distinguishing ministry by its locale of operation so much as seeking to classify various opportunities that present themselves.

Short-Term Service

There are now several avenues of very acceptable service open for consideration. The Peace Corps, VISTA, Youth Corps, Crossroads Africa, Operation Beaver — all of these and many more are dramatizing the fact that Christian youth can commit themselves to short-term service on a number of different fronts of Christian action. Most of these tours of duty are fitted in between the end of the young adult's formal education and his settlement in a job or vocation. A young doctor and his wife volunteer for two years to go to a developing country as soon as he has com-

[5] Peter L. Berger, *A Rumor of Angels* (New York: Doubleday & Company, Inc., 1969), p. 120.

pleted his internship. He has never seriously contemplated a life's vocation on the "mission field," but he is able to make a significant contribution for those two years.

Short-term service is becoming a very attractive alternative to a great many youth and ought to be kept prominently to the fore as a viable vehicle of Christian expression in ministry. The older tendency to look upon anything less than life commitment as somewhat suspect is being overcome. The one thing that needs emphasis over and over again is that God created the church to be the vehicle of expression in the world whereby his salvation may be made known and the person of Christ may be revealed. The "people of God," that community which is a new community, seeks to extend the redemptive activity of its God into all the world.

Long-Term Service

Sensitive Christians have always tried to keep firmly in mind their Lord's first invitation to the disciples and his last command to them. In John 1:39 he invited them to *come*. "Come and see." In Mark 16:15 his words are recorded *"Go . . . and preach"* (Italics mine). It is said that Bishop Azaiah exhorted the people of his diocese to come for confirmation and to place their hands on their heads and to repeat the words of Paul, "Woe to me if I do not preach the gospel!" (1 Corinthians 9:16). Such a confession sums up the basic attitude of the church which has heard and which is ready to engage itself in obedient service.

It would be a serious distortion of fact if the impression were conveyed that the *mission* program of the church is insignificant. There are still thousands of persons working abroad, away from their own lands, who are there as representatives of the church of Jesus Christ. As we have tried to indicate elsewhere, there are no longer any clear delineations between sending nations and receiving nations, between those who give and those who get. Instead, a more reciprocal relationship has developed, and it is a virtual certainty that this trend will not only continue but will become the rule rather than the exception.

Conditions of political climate and ideology have made necessary the withdrawal of the foreign missionaries from some lands, such as Burma. In others there is a movement toward the indigenization of the church, and the missionary is becoming a consultant rather than a primary practitioner, as in India. In others, such as Kenya, foreign personnel are being invited to serve for a specific period of time, working under a master plan conceived and administered by local councils of churches. For the foreseeable future it is likely that large numbers of persons will be called upon to minister in the mission of the church abroad.

The nature of missions has changed. With the emergence of the Third World and the ceaseless search within the developing nations for self-determination, there has come a new milieu. It is within this context that the Christian mission must learn to work. Persons contemplating a career in mission on one of the six continents would be well advised to consult the *International Review of Mission* and other journals to catch the sense of these developments. One example may be cited here to clarify the kinds of possibilities open and their theological implications.

In a recent issue of the *International Review of Mission* the Rev. G. M. Setiloane compares "The Missionary and His Task — at Edinburgh and Today." [6] In 1910 the "Mission" of the church was closely akin to being Western as the missionaries went East to Africa and Asia. "Today 'Mission' has become, — No, not yet! — should be — the business of every Christian person in the world, no matter from what race or continent." [7] It is no longer meaningful to speak of "Christian" countries as opposed to non-Christian; there needs rather to be a kind of "cross-fertilization" among all lands in which Christians dwell.

In 1910 the main character attributes required for an effective missionary were docility, gentleness, sympathy, and sensitivity, but now the requirements are phrased differently. "We want you to come to us as people, accepting us equally as people." [8] The concepts of leadership have changed; persons are needed who

[6] G. M. Setiloane," The Missionary and His Task — at Edinburgh and Today," *International Review of Mission,* vol. 59, no. 233 (January, 1970), pp. 55-66.

[7] *Ibid.,* p. 56.

[8] *Ibid.,* p. 58.

can be content "reacting sensitively and with integrity to God-given opportunities." [9]

The 1910 Report of Edinburgh called for a probationary term of four to five years for the missionary. Of the more than one hundred missionary students of British and Continental origin interviewed in 1969 at a Missionary Training Center, not one was ready to commit himself or herself for a life term of service.[10] Perhaps a balance needs to be struck between *short terms* and *long terms* of commitment. Both are needed in order to provide the maximum opportunities for all persons who are ready to respond to the need in the world.

Today we are confronted with the *mission of the whole church to the whole world*.

> Christ's commission (Matthew 28:19) is to "all nations," — there are none too big, too advanced, too "civilized" to receive it; none *only senders*, none *only receivers*. The humble teaching of the Early Church is that material assistance (dollars and sterling) was sent from the "Mission Field" to Jerusalem (1 Corinthians 16).[11]

MINISTRIES IN THE CITIES

A number of kinds of ministry are being tried in cities where established churches seem to have lost touch with the masses of people attracted to the great metropolitan areas. These ministries are truly experimental and provisional and what is written about them today may not be true tomorrow. But these examples suggest the scope of work being done and the opportunities for service that do exist.

The Coffee House Ministry

"The Purple Orb," the "Third Ear," "The Place," and "The Fish" are all names used to distinguish coffee house ministries as they have developed here and there across the land. One of the best known and most durable is the "Potter's House" in Washington, D.C., and we shall look at it at more length because it has been well documented and has some distinctive

[9] *Ibid.*, p. 60.
[10] *Ibid.*, pp. 60-61.
[11] *Ibid.*, p. 65.

features about it. Some of the material which follows has appeared in the book already cited.[12]

The Church of the Saviour, in Washington, D.C., has as its major outpost the ministry of the Potter's House. In order to understand the work of the Potter's House, which is a form of coffee house ministry, it is necessary to look first at the church itself.

The Church of the Saviour is a relatively small congregation of persons possessed by a burning desire to make church relevant to the life of twentieth-century Washington, the capital of the United States. The minister, N. Gordon Cosby, was convinced that his people were capable of discovering more creative and exciting ways of taking the message of the gospel into contemporary society. Accordingly he, in company with a few persons, began afresh to explore how this might be done. As far as possible, the old ways were ignored. The traditional trappings of much of the institutional church were rejected. Even the chosen place of meeting was a house in the inner city, selected because it was in the midst of the city, and not because it was commodious, spacious, or gracious. The founders agreed that the Church of the Saviour could not be content merely to exist for its own sake; it had to exist for the sake of the kingdom of God. The common accusations against the traditional church, "too much talk and too little action," were not to be applicable here. This local congregation would be mobilized for action.

Nine persons were received into membership of the church in the founding group. The commitment to which they pledged themselves includes their affirmations:

> I come today to join a local expression of the Church, which is the body of those on whom the call of God rests to witness to the grace and truth of God.
>
> I recognize that the function of the Church is to glorify God in adoration and sacrificial service, and to be God's missionary to the world, bearing witness to God's redeeming grace in Jesus Christ.
>
> I believe as did Peter that Jesus is the Christ, the Son of the Living God.
>
> I unreservedly and with abandon commit my life and destiny to Christ,

[12] See Elizabeth O'Connor, *Call to Commitment* (New York: Harper & Row, Publishers, 1963).

promising to give Him a practical priority in all the affairs of life. I will seek first the Kingdom of God and His Righteousness.

I commit myself, regardless of the expenditures of time, energy, and money to becoming an informed, mature Christian. . . .[13]

The brochure on the new church rightly warned

about a demanding way of life. . . . It is dangerous because you may find yourself digging with a shovel, or tracing current theologies, or reading the Bible, or changing your job . . . all life will be different and every sphere of one's existence involved in the change.[14]

The three-fold task of the church, teaching, proclamation, and service, is evident here. As the church builds up its own people to love and to serve, so it is called to evangelize through service. The Potter's House was to be a coffee house, and the medium of evangelism in the House was to be the common life of the Church of the Saviour. It was agreed that the House would serve as an art center and would be attractive to all persons of the area, especially artists, musicians, and craftsmen. Almost from its inception, it found a ready clientele. A corps of diligent people found their goals and commitments to service more than fully satisfied in this setting.

Any effective ministry of the type described here calls for a careful analysis both of the needs of the community and the resources that are at hand to meet these needs. The coffee house at best is a vehicle of expression. In some places it expresses itself clearly and with meaning; in other places it tends to degenerate into "just another gathering place."

An Experiment in the Inner City

The Church of the Holy Trinity is an Anglican parish located in the center of the business district of Toronto, Ontario. The ancient Trinity Square is surrounded by warehouses and other old buildings which, once impressive, are now weary with age. The one-hundred-year-old church has stood as a fortress in the midst of the commerce around it. Not many residents are within easy reach, and those who still commute are a diverse lot. As the people of the congregation looked at themselves in an attempt

[13] *Ibid.,* p. 20.
[14] *Ibid.,* p. 21.

to become more relevant and alive, they began to focus on their common beliefs in Christ and the fellowship of his people and they resolved to become outward looking as well as inward looking.

Changes did not come easily but as a new sense of direction developed, there came also a new willingness to risk and to become involved. Out of this came a number of rather bold ventures designed to get some windows in those "bastille-like walls."

Buildings adjacent to the church, long vacant, were commandeered for parish purposes. The sanctuary, after a great deal of soul searching, has been given over to purposes other than worship, and even the formal worship has been opened to non-traditional forms. Another avenue of service arrived on the doorstep in the form of a number of young men who had chosen to leave their homeland rather than be conscripted into a war in which they did not believe. Reading rooms and lounges for these and others were established, and a book room was opened to complement the Art Gallery and workshops across the street, also under church sponsorship. There are within walking distance of the church, derelicts, vagrants, prostitutes, alcoholics, addicts, and homosexuals. The people of Holy Trinity became aware of them and began to work to meet them in their community. Scadding House, a drop-in center, was established; a distress center to provide counseling for individuals seeking help became a reality; a Day Care Center to meet the needs of the children of families in substandard housing areas reached those whose lives were barren and deprived; Friendship Center, away from the square proper, found ways of ministering to a district afflicted with all the social diseases of the overcrowded inner city.

Most of these ministries are experimental. Constant evaluation is necessary to prevent the dissipation of the spiritual resources and to prevent even a good new thing from becoming separated from the essential reason for the church's existence.

Ministry in Industry

Because certain people in the church are convinced that the gospel has relevance to more than the individual, a great many attempts are being made which are addressed to structures. Ministries are pushing out into urban life in all directions — speaking to the politicians, the social scientists, the health science professions, to business and industry, and more. These sorties are based upon the confident hope that the Christian gospel can become effective at all levels of society. As George Younger, of New York, has stated it:

> Because the resistance of sin, both in persons and in the city at large, is so strong, the Christian hope possesses a relevance that surpasses any simple social optimism. Knowing that the power of sin has been broken in Christ, yet realizing that the complete fulfillment of the city of God has not yet been reached, the Christian is able to plan and to labor in hope. His hope is founded not on his own efforts nor on the efficacy of his strategies and plans, no matter how carefully drawn. Ultimately his hope is based on the power of God to redeem a broken and disobedient creation, to realize within the life of the metropolitan area some of the life of the city of God.[15]

The Detroit Industrial Mission is probably beyond the stage where it likes to be called experimental; yet even there, as the life of that great industrial complex ebbs and flows, the ministry of the "Mission" changes with it. Industrial ministries aim to become a sounding board for industrial plants in the area of decision making. The activities are directed toward both "Union" and "Management" and are beamed at the processes rather than at the individuals. On the assumption that decisions are made from the point of view of efficiency and economy on the one hand, and of reasonable working conditions and remuneration on the other, the ministry to industry shows its concern with the way such decisions are made. The insights and values inherent in a Christian evaluation of men will not be overlooked in a struggle to make decisions equitable for all concerned. Ministries to Industry not only put the voice of the church on the industrial scene but also provide much needed feedback to the local churches helping them to become aware of the tensions, problems, turmoil, and the potentialities of that complex world.

---

[15] George D. Younger, *The Church and Urban Power Structure* (Philadelphia: The Westminster Press, 1963), p. 67. Copyright © MCMLXIII, W. L. Jenkins. Used by permission.

Action Training

A number of training centers in North America have formed an Action Training Coalition to provide a training resource in urban issues for church professionals. Action training and strategies for social change are offered as well as skill training in organization development, group process, community and issues analysis, confrontation, and problem solving. Urban studies deal with racism, church renewal, and change through labs, lectures, simulation games, and direct engagement.

A few of these centers, CUT (Center for Urban Training) in Toronto, MUST (Metropolitan Urban Service Training) in New York City, and MAP (Metropolitan Associates of Philadelphia) in Philadelphia have interesting acronyms as titles. But all are centers similar in their purpose, which is to help the church professional to become aware of the dynamics of his society through action and involvement so he may better minister to society out of that enhanced understanding. The prime purpose of these centers is to train people to work more effectively in their chosen vocation. A few will want to make action training a ministry; however, this is not a primary purpose of these centers.

WORKER PRIESTS – TENT-MAKING MINISTRIES

These two titles appear side by side because they depict very similar approaches to ministry. Some people have felt so strongly the pull to get out of the narrow, relatively cribbed and cabined ministry they have known that they have taken secular employment and have "gone underground." The thinking behind such a move is to take one's place on the assembly line, in the mart, or in the factory and to live out the implications of the Christian presence there. From that base one can naturally infiltrate all the structures of human life and society. There may not be the same opportunities for preaching, but there are opportunities for the steady, effectual working of a committed life.

Because the church has always sought to help persons to be fully Christian in all their relationships, theoretically one should not be able to discern much difference between a worker-priest, a part-time minister, and a Christian by any other name. We do know, however, that we have frequently found our treasure to be in earthen vessels and our influence has not been as effective as we might have hoped.

Another extension or form of this tent-making ministry is developing in places where several members of a congregation bind themselves together to become the ministry of the church, each of them serving part time. Probably all of them will have secular employment. One will be responsible for preaching and leadership of worship, one for Christian education, one for pastoral care, one for missions and outreach. Because there are necessary calls of an emergency nature in any sizable congregation, it may be wise to have one of the ministers "on call" at all times. He may be self-employed, or almost so, in order to be flexible enough to respond as needed. Such a team approach calls for careful planning and coordination. It is already being practiced successfully and may very well be one of the viable forms for tomorrow's ministry. Essentially what is looked for was expressed by Hendrik Kraemer:

> The issue is that both laity and ministry stand in need of a new vision of the nature and calling of the Church and their *distinctive places* in it, which means conversion and reformation for the whole Church, laity as well as ministry. Renewal is always based on repentance and new commitment and dedication to the fundamental basis of Christian existence, viz. God's craving for the collaboration with Him of His whole Church, in His work of redemption.[16]

On the evidence of Ephesians 4:13-16, Arnold Come sees the hope for the "abolition" of the laity so "the whole community will participate more fully in the inner life of the church, and thereby receive the spiritual nourishment necessary for maturation in the faith and knowledge of the Son of God." [17] As the traditional concept of the clergy is abolished, they are freed to "maintain a deeper and more natural participation in the life of the world, and thereby the whole Christian community may

---

[16] Hendrik Kraemer, *A Theology of the Laity* (Philadelphia: The Westminster Press, 1958), p. 95. © Hendrik Kraemer 1958. Used by permission.

[17] Arnold B. Come, *Agents of Reconciliation* (Philadelphia: The Westminster Press, 1960) p. 167 (Hardbound edition). Copyright © MCMLX, W. L. Jenkins. Used by permission.

more realistically and effectively take part in the ministry of reconciliation to the world." [18]

Come concludes then: "the ministries designed to build up the
church in size and quality are of *first* importance, but the ministry of reconciliation to the world is of *ultimate* importance in
the being and calling of the church." [19]

[18] *Ibid.*, p. 167.
[19] *Ibid.*, p. 169.

6   . . . All the Difference

> "And they remembered that God was their strength. . . ."
>
> Psalm 78:35

In one of the detective stories written by Agatha Christie, Hercule Poirot is asked by a teenage girl: "Is there such a place as the 'brave new world' hailed by Miranda in Shakespeare's *The Tempest?*" "There is always a brave new world," he replies, "but only for very special people. The lucky ones. The ones who carry the making of that world within themselves."

As we have looked at the wide ranging possibilities for Christian ministry, we have constantly kept in mind the ever widening scene wherein such ministry may be performed. Perhaps we could sum up the kinds of expectations that are emerging by looking at one more type of ministry. It was featured in the *United Church Observer* under the title "New Kind of Parish, New Kind of Minister." [1]

Tom Elden is the chaplain for the International Airport in Vancouver, British Columbia. As he seeks to serve the personnel of this fast-moving industrial complex, he quickly becomes aware of the fact that this is not an easy place to minister. The outside observers see the speed, the glamour, and the thrills that aviation can provide. What they do not see, however, are the problems connected with moving quickly through time zones and international boundaries, the pressures and responsibilities, the weird working and leisure schedules, and the extremes of affluence and waste (unused meals dumped at the end of each flight, etc.). "In

[1] "New Kind of Parish: New Kind of Minister," *United Church Observer*, July, 1970.

the world of the airport, an indifference to the world outside is almost inevitable." [2] The worker in an airport occupation cannot easily escape from this captive environment.

It was not always Tom Elden's intention to become an airport chaplain. Tom came late into the chaplaincy. For nine years he had done part-time theological studies squeezed in between regular flight assignments. As he neared the completion of these studies, a baggage handler approached him one day and startled him with: "Are you going to leave here and take an ordinary church somewhere after you're ordained?" Elden admitted that this was in fact his intention. The reply came back: "You're crazy! — We need you here!"

A good deal of reflection forced Elden to realize that in all of his years around an airport he had heard almost nothing about Christian convictions and that now people were seeking him out for counseling and discussions that before had seemed taboo under ordinary conditions. "What they wanted, he concluded, was 'someone they could think of as representing God,' someone who could crack the taboo by his presence." [3]

Airport chaplaincies are now in operation in Miami, Atlanta, New Orleans, Oklahoma City, Boston, San Francisco, and New York City, to compile an incomplete list. The world is the parish, and the kind of ministry suited to that parish must be geared to today.

We began in chapter 1 by saying "Yes" to ministry. We saw that the call of the Eternal to his servants is still issued in strange, devious, and yet wonderful ways. The question occurs and recurs: "What is God doing in the current world order?" That question triggers question after question, not the least of which is: "How and where can I join in this work?" The call for the peacemakers, for those who will serve justice, show mercy, and love righteousness, for all who will be enrolled in *this community* (the church), continues to go forth with all of its original energy and urgency.

As we have seen, there are almost countless ways in which persons may make this response to such a call.

[2] *Ibid.,* p. 13.
[3] *Ibid.,* pp. 13-14.

William Overholt, Protestant chaplain at Boston University, has phrased it this way: "To make a vocational choice in our time is to say 'yes' to what God is doing and to resolve to respond by enlisting in what he is doing to meet the needs of a desperate world." [4] The conclusion of Chaplain Overholt's pamphlet sums it up:

> The young person who chooses to invest his life in such tasks has a vocation which will give his life purpose and meaning, will enrich him in the fellowship of his fellow-volunteers and in the satisfaction of dealing with important issues, not just trivial and distracting tasks. [5]

For those who choose to engage in such ministries a great fraternity of co-workers stands ready to work with them. Many are the opportunities for cooperation, consultation, and occasions to pursue common goals and aspirations. This book has not dealt with matters of financial remuneration, because the range varies too widely for any figures to be meaningful. Seminaries and colleges are striving manfully to create the kinds of curricula that will permit men and women to equip themselves as adequately as possible to enter the widest range of ministries. More and more institutions and centers are looking to the providing of continuing education for all who have dedicated themselves to minister. It is becoming common practice for local churches and other sponsoring agencies to allow two to three weeks of study time each year (over and above regular vacation periods) to permit its personnel to update and complement their basic skills and approaches to their work. A few have even adopted the practice of universities of providing for a sabbatical study leave every seven to ten years of a person's service.

As far as the New Testament record is concerned, ministry, in its meaning of service or work, is first of all the responsibility and privilege of all the people of God. It is this responsibility that we are called upon to share by engaging in acts that will make manifest the love and concern of God for his creation. Someone has said that the ministry of the church consists then of "its worship, its self-giving love, and its testimony concerning the re-

---

[4] William Overholt, *Choosing a Life Work* (pamphlet), p. 16.

[5] *Ibid.*, p. 26.

conciling power of Jesus Christ." The response to this continuing challenge brings excitement and vitality into one's life. How will God have us serve here and now as his chosen people, to be his instruments to seek to communicate to his world the once-for-all reconciling act in Christ Jesus?

As Robert Frost has it:

> Two roads diverged in a wood, and I —
> I took the one less traveled by,
> And that has made all the difference.[6]

It will indeed make all the difference and you are cordially invited to make your choice.

[6] From "The Road Not Taken" from *The Poetry of Robert Frost,* edited by Edward Connery Latham. Copyright 1916, © 1969 by Holt, Rinehart and Winston, Inc. Copyright 1944 by Robert Frost. Reprinted by permission of Holt, Rinehart and Winston, Inc.

Appendix

(Adapted from Chapter 9 in "The Minister's Job" by Albert Palmer.)

This is not an objective test than can be "scored." It can be useful in helping a student to evaluate his own potential in terms of a well-rounded profile of self-measurement. In some instances the student might be wise to check his own assessment with a counselor in whom he confides.

Personal Appearance

1. Unusual physical traits — such as might interfere with one's effective performance of ministry.
2. Physical vitality — energy.
3. Quality of voice — a voice pitched too high or too low can interfere with communication.
4. Speech — impediments or defects may need remedial training.
5. General dress — neatness and personal habits.

Temperament

1. Intelligence — the demands of an academic program require reasonable learning abilities.
2. Temperament and disposition.
3. Judgment.
4. Ability to learn.
5. Attitude toward responsibility.
6. Ability for independent action coupled with an awareness of the potential within the actions of other persons.

Social Qualities

1. Ability to establish relationships with people and to work cooperatively with others — especially those with divergent views.
2. Basic courtesy and the observance of accepted social customs.
3. A sense of humor.
4. Punctuality.
5. Insight into social issues and problems.
6. Capacity for leadership.
7. A capacity to manage personal financial affairs.

The Religious Life

1. A sound attitude toward self and others.
2. A genuine commitment to an experience of God in Christ.
3. An attitude of openness and tolerance toward those of other faiths.
4. A commitment to a devotional attitude that is consistent with a daily profession of faith.
5. A growing experience of love and of loving.
6. A willingness to become obedient to the demands that such a faith makes in terms of ministry, service, and dedication.[1]

[1] Adapted from Albert W. Palmer, *The Minister's Job* (New York: Harper & Row, Publishers, 1949), pp. 79-90.

Selected bibliography

Hiltner, Seward, *Ferment in the Ministry.* Nashville: Abingdon Press, 1969.

Mullin, Thomas J., *The Renewal of the Ministry.* Nashville: Abingdon Press, 1963.

O'Connor, Elizabeth, *Call to Commitment.* New York: Harper & Row, Publishers, 1963.

Raines, Robert A., *The Secular Congregation.* New York: Harper & Row, Publishers, 1968.

Reitz, Rudiger, *The Church in Experiment.* Nashville: Abingdon Press, 1969.

Snyder, Ross, *Young People and Their Culture.* Nashville: Abingdon Press, 1969.

Index

Books on